GLORY STORIES

I Was a Human Test Dummy

Margo Clark

Margo Clark
Jan. 29:11

MARGO CLARK

Cover designed by Lara Lee

LSGS Publishing © 2014

ISBN: 1-500-444-83-9

ISBN-13: 978-1-500444-83-9

"When you pass through the waters, I will be with you: and when you pass through the rivers they will not sweep over you. When you walk through the fire, you will not be burned; the flames will not set you ablaze."

(Is. 43:2)

DEDICATION

I would like to dedicate this book to the Lord Jesus Christ, who has proven himself to be my rock, my sanity, my hope, my healer and the one who has loved me with an everlasting love. He has delivered my life from the jaws of death and surrounded me with his powerful presence, and he has given his angels charge over me. He has given me hope where there seemed to be no sunrise. I stand on the rock, the only firm foundation, who has filled me with joy. My life is an ode of gratitude to the King of Kings and the Lord of Lords.

I also give incredible thanks to my husband Mike and my son Matt who have walked through this unique journey with me, exhibiting the extraordinary love of Jesus to me.

ACKNOWLEDGEMENTS

The pen and I have had a fond relationship since high school when I began writing poetry. I have discovered over the years, the cathartic value of journaling. When my pen sat idle, my thoughts churned, yearning for release. Several years ago, I became aware of the fact that I was pregnant with several books. As I attempted to seriously undertake the project, I encountered much opposition in the form of physical ailments. In July of the past year, I attended a healing service and received a healing of my most vicious and persistent migraines. This opened the door and I began to write.

I owe a great deal of gratitude to encouragers along the way. First of all, my Lord Jesus Christ for enabling the stories to be a reality that needs to be shared for his glory and for such a merciful and miraculous healing of the majority of migraine headaches that enabled me to concentrate and write. Secondly, the help and encouragement of my patient husband, Mike Clark, who has opened the world of computers to me and given me the confidence to tangle with the machine.

I appreciate the vote of confidence from my son, Matt Clark, who has given me permission to share the stories and who first helped me to tackle the challenges and my personal fear of the computer. I appreciate his humor and patience as he would tell me that I looked like a frightened kitty, jumping on the keys. He confidently assured me that the computer would not blow up if I hit an incorrect key. I have learned that lesson, although I confess that I still am prone to jumping hands!

I remain eternally grateful to many of my doctors who have shared their expertise over the years attempting to heal and help '*the little engine that could.*' They have been the recipients of many prayers.

I want to thank a longtime friend Pat Gilliss who encouraged me to write and helped me with the nuts and bolts of publishing.

Also I appreciate my dear friend, Angela Dion, for exhorting me to write and for teaching me over the years. In addition, I appreciate the encouragement of my longtime friend, Beth Vogt who is wise beyond her years. I would also like to express my gratitude to Lara Lee who has designed the beautiful cover and helped me with technology. I am also incredibly thankful for Kathy Dobyns, who has patiently edited my chapters, challenging me over these past months. We have shared many memories, humor and life journeys.

I know that I would not have been able to accomplish this feat, were it not for my spiritual cheerleaders, and life-long friends: Lyn, Jenifer, Angela, Jennifer, Linda Sue, and Liz. I am blessed beyond measure to claim you as friends. You are my Jonathans.

ENDORSEMENTS

"Margo Clark is an articulate, insightful author. She is a born again Christian whose talk matches her walk. This book is incredible. If you doubt that Jesus is in charge, you should definitely read this book. It is amazing all the obstacles and horrendous events that have beset Margo. However, she gives God all the glory and He protected her in every event, which just increased her faith in her Almighty Saviour. Margo is a spiritual giant who has time to really be there for all who call on her for help, me included. Many times I have called Margo in a panic, she dropped what she was doing, and gave me her full attention along with wisdom, insight, and spiritual encouragement. I am privileged to call her my deep forever friend. This book is a must read for all to read, and it is aptly entitled Glory Stories. *"Greater is He who is in YOU than he who is in the world." (1 John 4:4).*

—Jenifer Clark, Satellite Oceanographer, http://users.erols.com/gulfstrm/ Lecturer at USNA, Tall Ships in Bermuda, Newport to Bermuda Yacht Race, Marion to Bermuda Yacht Race; Ocean/weather support for Diana Nyad for her swim from Cuba to Florida; Ocean/weather router for Erden Eruc (Around and Over) around the world row as well as Tori Murden's record breaking row across the Atlantic; Ocean race clients included Heraldo Rivera, Hugh Downs, Roy Disney, Steve Fossett, David Povich (Maury's brother), and Walter Cronkite.

"This book reveals how a woman with many physical, mental, and spiritual stresses in her lifetime, has clearly survived because of her strong and unbreakable belief in our heavenly God.

I am in awe and somewhat envious that her strong faith is unwavering in spite of overwhelming odds during her lifetime. Her journal thoughts at the end of each chapter are very useful for the reader to reflect on their own beliefs, convictions, and walk with God."

— Tommy Higgins, Author of How Far is it From Richmond to Heaven

"As I have read the words of this talented author, I was so moved emotionally. I groaned, smiled, frowned, and cried. As she was able to overcome the next obstacle, I felt relief, when she was taking the fall, I felt like I went down with her. I am especially partial to the across the table format. It invites the reader to relax, and enjoy. I have known the spiritual walk of this writer many years, however, this is the most personally I have ever known her. Margo has a true talent to project her feeling fully in her writing. You won't be disappointed purchasing this book. You will be blessed far beyond the cost. She lives this life openly, and excitedly. What a beautiful faith to share with the world! God's blessings upon you, Margo Clark."

—*Pat Gilliss, author of:* You Asked God For WHAT? *and* No More Crumbs, Eat What You Will From the Master's Table

"You are about to read the story on one of God's demonstrations of His glorious grace. Margo is a friend to all she meets. That friendship includes a prayer partnership, a source of encouragement and wisdom from someone who walks with God. Margo has given us a gift in telling her God-story. She truly gives us glimpses of the glorious grace our Maker has provided for all. You will enjoy the book—and be drawn to the good God of Heaven and Earth, who also wants to be your Friend."

— *Dave Huffman, Senior Pastor of South Potomac Church*

CONTENTS

MARGO CLARK

INTRODUCTION

ow do you have the courage to get behind the wheel of a car again?

This is a question that I frequently hear as I share the events of my driving career these many years.

In reality, having been severely injured in twelve car accidents can be viewed as shock, tragedy, or bad luck. Our minds and souls seek a method of coping with such life events. We are left questioning the whys of terrible situations. Many people find escape from the unfathomable through humor. I have one dear friend who has dubbed me "a human test dummy."

Hind sight is 100% as I view each of these trials from the perspective of God's master plan for my life.

As I look back at many instances of mayhem, I'm ever more convinced of the Lord's hand on my life, despite overwhelming forces.

Step back in time with me. Imagine rose colored glasses, lilacs in bloom, the sun kissing the land, birds singing, the merriment of spring and the crescendo of laughter echoing in a young girl's soul. Such were the reasonable expectations of a five year old viewing life with stars in her eyes and hope in her heart.

Somewhere in the ensuing years, the realities of life distorted the dream. The Disney expectations were harder to hold on to and at times it looked like the Big Bad Wolf was winning.

The stories that I will be sharing in this book are told not through rose colored glasses but through the soft lens of decades of reality and the solid hope that has sustained me and has assured me that the Big Bad Wolf doesn't win in the end. The real hero of the story is the Lord Jesus Christ, my Prince, my King, and my Hero.

The rose colored glasses are an illusion, a dreamer's utopian wish-world. I prefer the winners' bleachers because as a Christian, I know how the story ends.

This book is the result of a radical response to the initial question of how I could ever summon the courage to get behind the wheel of a car again.

It involved 'facing the giants' of PTSD (post-traumatic stress disorder), of refusing to become an emotional and physical invalid, and of just how to continue when both terror and overwhelming pain were threatening to cripple and consume my life.

This book is about hope for the hopeless: those who have come through unimaginable nightmares and are treading water and believe their lungs are filling with water and their legs are exhausted, those who are questioning if God cares and will rescue them.

I have written this book to encourage so many women and men who are feeling overwhelmed, and are experiencing battle fatigue.

As I think of hope, I remember one particular spring day when I was leaving school quite fatigued after teaching an entire day with a migraine headache. There had been a particularly nasty storm over the school. At dismissal, there was a pause in the downpour as everyone hurried to exit the parking lot. As I sat in the line I observed the dark, ominous clouds surrounding us.

All at once, there was a parting of the clouds and a rainbow broke through and the end of the rainbow was directly in front of us. The trees were shimmering and scintillating with the colors of the rainbow. I pulled over to just drink in the beauty. My heart beat quickly with delight as I watched each color-drenched leaf dance in the breeze. No, there was no pot of gold, but I believe that the Lord was showing me that there was hope right in the center of the storm. I held on to that spectacular memory as I continued to struggle with multiple figurative tornadoes swirling in my life. I believe that the Lord provides rainbows of hope in the tornadoes of life.

My desire is that the reader will discover or rediscover hope despite personal persistent disappointments, heartaches, frustration, depression and despair that may be overwhelming them, obscuring the sunlight. I know this journey quite will. Come with me as I recount many memories of God's rainbows in tornadoes. He does have rainbows for each of us, despite our present drenching deluge. Let's chase rainbows together.

I believe that as a result of reading this book, the reader will be able to search the Word of God for answers and hope when life makes no sense, and an insidious inner voice whispers that you are a loser who will never win. When darkness crawls up to choke you, there is a Light and a Hero-Savior. His name is Jesus. Keep searching. Keep reaching for help. Don't isolate. Don't ever give up.

God's Word states,

> "'For I know the plans I have for you,' declares the Lord, 'Plans to prosper you and not to harm you, plans to give you hope and a future.'"

> (Jer. 29:11)

"Though he slay me, yet will I hope in him."

(Job 13:15)

"But he knows the way I take: when he has tested me, I will come forth as gold."

(Job 23:10)

"This poor man cried and the Lord heard him, and saved him out of all his troubles."

(Ps. 34:6)

"The Lord will sustain him on his sickbed and restore him from his bed of illness."

(Ps. 41:3)

I will be sharing accounts of the Lord's faithfulness throughout my life, showcased through inexplicable deliverance from dangers, and my life ultimately having been spared through the Lord's almighty intervention.

The Scriptures shared in the following stories are ones that I had read in the late 1970s when I became acquainted with the Word of God. Little did I know that the very Scriptures that were captivating my soul would become a lifeline for me as I searched for the meaning of a life that seemed to be following convoluted paths.

My prayer is that these pages will bless the reader with hope as each one trusts the Designer and Refiner of our lives.

TESTIMONY

L et's take some time to get acquainted. I was born in 1946, the youngest of five children. I was the only child in our family born in the hospital. My father was a government sheet metal worker. My mom was a retired school teacher who bore and raised us all despite a crippled and shriveled right arm.

When I was three years old we moved from Greenbelt to Morningside, Maryland. Andrews Air Force Base had just opened and my father transferred from Bowling Air Force Base to Andrews where, as shop foreman, he maintained aircraft, including Air Force One. While on Bowling Air Force Base, he fitted the plane to accommodate President Roosevelt's wheelchair and was given an award for his industrious achievement. My dad received many awards for his creative inventions including a personal gift from the Queen of England. He was one of the most ingenious men I have ever known.

I was the only child in our family who received an entire Catholic school education. Mt. Calvary in Forestville was where I was taught by the School Sisters of Notre Dame, who greatly influenced the direction of my life. Following graduation from the eighth grade, I attended Villa Regina Academy, a boarding school for girls who wanted to become nuns.

High School was a wonderful time of deep friendships, hard work and the cyclically ambivalent agony of both leaving home and leaving friends for holidays and vacations.

Ever since the first grade, I had wanted to become a nun. They were mesmerizing role models, who seemed to float rather than walk

5

through the church. They were strict teachers and effective disciplinarians.

During high school, I excelled at languages, especially Latin. Our principal was our surrogate mother and spiritual coach. She was a totally inspiring and godly woman who was also my Latin teacher. I managed to win awards nationally under her dynamic instruction. During these years we learned to sing, play sports and create our own fun. We experienced community while we were still teenagers. Our lifestyle was that of a rigorously spiritual R.O.T.C. We look back and laugh, frequently saying that the marines had nothing on us.

Following graduation in 1964 I entered the Motherhouse, Villa Assumpta, which was located on the same campus as our high school in Baltimore, MD. One year of college as a postulant prepared us for the following year of spiritual boot-camp, called the novitiate. It was an austere year of cloister that qualified us for taking our three vows of poverty, chastity and obedience. We were only allowed to speak two hours a day. We were put through many archaic, medieval tests. Those who didn't pass the rigors of the cloister were disqualified and told to leave. Upon completion of that year, vows were taken during an elaborately liturgical ceremony. New names were given to each of us. My name was changed from Margo Helen Benden to Sister Margo Marie.

Two weeks later, most of us were sent out on mission to teach, after having had methods courses over the two year period and then a two week crash course on classroom technique. I was sent to a convent in Ybor City, Tampa, Florida to teach the fourth grade. Once there, I was mentored daily by an older sister who helped me segue into teaching and mission life. I also taught some fifth and sixth grade classes and multiple classes in music. While there I also attended evening classes at the University of South Florida. I spent the next two years there, enthralled with teaching, the Cuban culture and the novelties of Florida.

Several of us young sisters approached our superior (boss) and inquired if we could help the poverty stricken people surrounding our complex since we were finished teaching and home by 3:30. We were met with the stern reply, "If you wanted to do that, you should have become social workers." An explosion took place within my heart and mind. We knew that the woman living in a house on the street behind our convent was blind and had to sleep with a broom to keep the rats off her bed. Our convent was surrounded by those in dire need.

As a result of the Superior's comment to us, I remember wrestling with the teaching that as nuns, we were the Bride of Christ, which equaled the personification of love in my mind. This heightened my observation that the religious lifestyle seemed to destroy all that was spontaneous and loving. I noticed that in our convent, the older nuns lacked spontaneity and warmth and were quite rigid. There were a few exceptions, but I was observing the effects of legalism. Therefore, for the first time in my young life, I began to question all that I had been taught and automatically accepted.

What ensued were months of personal turmoil, panic, praying and searching. I decided to leave the convent after much drama within our convent, in which I found myself ostracized. I had to write to Rome for a dispensation from my vows. I had taken three year vows and after two years I made the extremely difficult decision to leave. At this time, leaving the convent was worse than getting a divorce in the Catholic Church. Not one nun in our group had left. As far as I knew, I was the first to leave. Most of us had been together in this venture since we were thirteen years old.

My world was being torn apart. The fabric of our country was also being shredded as a result of the Viet Nam war and the assassination of Dr. Martin Luther King. Our convent had just been entrenched in the middle of the terrifying, ensuing riots. I was watching my entire world burn that night. By God's grace, we were not harmed that evening. The devastating chaos surrounding us was an appropriate picture of what was happening in my heart. Before I left Florida, I went into the chapel and prayed, "Jesus Christ, You are the Son of God and I'm going to find you and I don't know what else is true."

I left Florida by train for the Motherhouse in Baltimore not knowing if my dispensation from my vows had been granted. I had decided to leave even if it had not been granted. This meant that I would have been ex-communicated from the Catholic Church and therefore would be going to hell. I was terrified, but no longer trusted theologians. I was determined to find the truth, to find absolutes. With my heart pounding, I spent what seemed like an eternity alone in a business office in the Motherhouse waiting for the hierarchical decision. Finally the door opened and an elderly nun approached me with papers in her hand. I breathed a great sigh of relief and changed into civilian clothes, ready to start another chapter of my life as I had two wonderful friends waiting outside in a 1968 Mustang convertible to take me to freedom.

My social life quickly evolved due to the existence of a Catholic young adult club in the District of Columbia. That is where I met the love of my life, Mike Clark, who had just returned from Viet Nam. One slow dance and I was swept off my feet. I felt incredibly cherished and protected in his wonderful arms.

We were married on June 13, 1970. I continued to worship in the Catholic church even though I disagreed with much of its theology. I was on a quest for truth. Shortly after coming home, I visited a large

Catholic bookstore in Washington D.C. and brought home about ten books dealing with doctrine and church history. I realized that the terror of damnation had controlled and consumed much of my life and I reasoned that freedom had to come by somehow attacking my deepest fears head on. During the next several years I continued to teach and study, personally feeling overwhelmed by the stresses of being an adult child of an alcoholic, a survivor of sexual abuse by seven different perpetrators, and a former nun, while simultaneously, dealing with the ravages of infertility and the urgency of searching for absolutes. During this time and process, I managed to logically demolish my entire theological foundation.

By 1975 I realized that our marriage was headed for trouble. I asked my husband to allow me to go to counseling since I had to regularly deal with the overwhelming presence of my father and unresolved issues in my life. He refused, not trusting therapists. Having been unable to discover absolutes in my life, I refused to trust any man, woman, or institution, especially the Church. Consequently, I decided to place all of my trust in myself. After all, I reasoned, the convent had never made a rule that I had not scrupulously kept. The problem was that eventually I failed my own standards which brought me to a place of complete disillusionment and hopelessness. As a result, one day I got into my car and started driving fast in a wooded area looking for the biggest tree I could find in order to end my life. As I began to dramatically increase my speed, I heard an audible, cashmere, warm, smiling voice that said, "If you do this, you're going to be face to face with Jesus Christ?" I immediately slowed down and thought "What was that?" Just as quickly I said, "No, I'm going to do this" and I began to accelerate. Again I heard the voice saying, "And then you're going to Hell?" I immediately slowed down and began to beat the steering wheel and shouted, "I don't know who's right, Jesus Christ or the Catholic church?" My heart was pounding, my hands sweating, my ears ringing and my mind was racing. I remember reasoning that if Jesus Christ was the Son of God, He couldn't lie. So I turned the car around to go back and opened a dusty Bible to read the four gospels and hopefully ascertain whether I could commit suicide and not be damned. I wasn't sure I could trust the rest of the Bible, and I remembered learning in grade school that John was the apostle of love, so I decided to start with the gospel of John.

All alone in my living room, I just happened to open the gospel of John to *John 10:27-28* which reads, *"My sheep listen to my voice (which I had just heard). I know them and they follow me. I give them eternal life and they shall never perish: no one can snatch them out of my hand."* Having heard those words, the terror that had controlled and gripped my life like a dark, crushing vice was gone. I distinctively remember the sensation of a heavy tarpaulin slipping from my head and body. I felt such a release. I sat forward in my chair looking at the ceiling praying, "If there's a formula prayer, I don't know it, but I'm telling you, I'm one of your sheep. Amen."

After that prayer, I couldn't stop reading the Scriptures. I was finally finding the answers I had so long hungered and searched for. *Jeremiah 29:13* states, *"You will seek me and find me when you seek me with all your heart."*

During the very same month the Lord was dealing with my husband who also prayed and received Jesus as his personal savior. We spent the next ten months like two children in a candy shop as we discovered and relished in the delights of the Word of God. At the end of that time frame, Mike's sister called us and realized that we had accepted the Lord into our hearts. She had been praying for us for over a year and told us about a little Bible chapel two miles from our home. We visited and stayed for the next thirteen years. Then, due to legalism within the church, Mike and I and four other couples started a new church in Southern Maryland called South Potomac Church. It sits on fifty acres of land and has ministered effectively to the local community. Today, by the grace of God, I find myself one of the older women of the church who is able to teach the younger women how to love their husbands, and to live a life pleasing to the Lord. My heart overflows with joy and thanksgiving to the holy Lord who constantly pursued me, stopping my destructive path, and faithfully restoring my heart through the years.

The Lord in his gracious mercy also gave us our only son, Matthew James Clark, after seventeen years of infertility, a miracle and testimony to so many people. The Lord gave us Matt at the last possible moment. After his birth, tests indicated a pre-cancerous condition and I quickly needed a complete hysterectomy.

A favorite verse of mine is *Is. 58:11.* which states: *"The Lord will guide you always; he will satisfy your needs in a sun-scorched land and will strengthen your frame. You will be like a well-watered garden, like a spring whose waters fail not."*

I worship my Lord Jesus Christ who has graciously brought my life full-circle. It doesn't get much better than this. To God be the glory!

WHAT VALUE—PAIN?

I f your mind is anything like mine, you have wrestled with both the problem and the value of pain. My questioning began as a young child. I didn't have to look far.

My mother was one of sixteen children. She was born in 1905 in the small coal mining town of Gallitzin, Pennsylvania. Her father was the superintendent of the mine and her mother was the local seamstress and midwife.

When my mother was beginning to crawl, one of her sisters picked her up by her right arm, dislocating the arm at the shoulder. Her mother began to notice a problem with the arm and took her to the local town doctor who happened to be an alcoholic. He dismissed my grandmother's fears, telling her that the arm was fine. So my mother was taken home and the problem was temporarily ignored.

Unwilling to accept his word, my grandmother eventually took my mother to a doctor in the adjoining town to have her arm evaluated. The doctor was aghast. He told my grandmother that the arm had simply been dislocated. However due to the delay in diagnosis and treatment, the damage was permanent. The muscles had atrophied. My mother would spend the rest of her life coping with a grotesquely crippled arm.

When she was a young woman my grandmother told her not to expect marriage because no man would want to marry someone who was crippled. Accepting this as truth, my mother became a school teacher in a one room school house where she would walk miles to school, and once there gather wood for the small wood burning stove to warm the ice-cold building and snow-covered children.

One St. Patrick's Day she agreed to go on a blind date initiated by another teacher. My mom was a gifted woman who had a beautiful operatic voice and loved to dance. The night was filled with singing Irish melodies, dancing, laughter and the beginning of my parent's courtship.

My father came from a family of fourteen children and had to quit school when he was twelve to go to work in the coal mines due to the death of his father. With nine mouths to feed, my dad became the surrogate father figure and bread winner.

Neither his mother nor most of his siblings came to my parent's wedding because Mom was crippled. My dad's mother said there was no way Mom could have children. *Jer. 29:11* states that the Lord has a plan for each of our lives and that it's a plan for good, not for evil, to give us a future and a hope. My mother lived that hope. Though she was physically crippled, she was a mighty woman who loved intensely and victoriously. She was also an amazing woman who exhibited great strength of character often displayed in dogged determination. She modeled perseverance. She once told me that the only thing she was not able to do as a parent was to work a zipper. To that, she conceded defeat!

Growing up and hearing the many New Testament stories of how Jesus healed so many people, I would pray daily for a miracle for my precious mother. Little did I know that my dad and older siblings' prayers were identical to mine.

One day when I was in the sixth grade, Mom told me that while she was hanging clothes to dry over the furnace grate, she had totally lifted her arm up to the clothes line above the grate for several seconds. Then her arm dropped and returned to its limp, non-functioning condition. She was misty-eyed and filled with wonder and elation as she related the miraculous incident.

I remember having such ambivalent emotions racing through my heart. I was thrilled for Mom, but I was also unsure of the Lord's motivation. Did he really care? Were my expectations of total healing unrealistic? The momentary miracle seemed capriciously cruel to me and I stopped praying for such a healing. My young heart was guarding itself from disappointment.

My mother lived to be eighty five. I tell people that she died an eighty five year old teenager. To her last breath, her humor, wit and smile permeated the air around her. She was a woman who exhaled joy, blessing everyone who knew her.

As I look back at her life and all those prayers, I have come to realize that the Lord was working a more magnificent miracle in our lives through my mother's infirmity than that of simply curing a paralyzed arm. All of us learned to pray and persevere in prayer, overcoming the prayer paralysis that occasionally could set in due to a divine delay. We learned to trust God's purposes even when they made no sense to us. We each were given tender hearts, sensitized by Mom's suffering, sensitized to the sufferings of others. Our characters were being formed by the hand of the potter himself.

My mother's inability to drive kept us in a small town setting where we developed lifelong friends. We learned to create our own fun. All of us learned the medicinal value of raucous laughter. Truly God wove the limitations of my mother's infirmity into an intricate pattern of blessings.

There are some people in life called heroes. My mother was a true heroine who graced those around her from a place of deepest faith and courage. She was an overcomer.

❧ JOURNALING ❧

1. *Do you believe that God has a plan for your life?*

2. *What evidence do you see of God's direction in your life?*

3. *Write Jer. 29:11. Memorize this verse in the translation of your choice.*

4. *Ask the Lord to show you his plan for your life.*

THE HAND OF GOD

Looking back over the events of my life, I am amazed at the protection provided for me from the womb. My mother had four children at home and I was the only child born in a hospital. The doctor was furious with her for not coming to him during the pregnancy. He sarcastically scolded her and asked her why she didn't wait until I was born to see him. Yet without any medical care during the pregnancy, I, like my four older siblings, was born without any birth defects. Except for my oldest brother, we were all small babies, weighing five pounds or less.

I loved being the youngest and having the security of older siblings was wonderful. Feeling protected, especially by my older brothers was such a gift. Also having one older sister who was an awesome seamstress, inspired me to learn to sew and create beauty around me. We are all aging these days, yet enjoying reasonable health and our parties are scenes of enviable fun.

I remember going horseback riding when I was young at the White Sands Beach Club in southern Maryland. This was our only regular family outing. I looked forward to summer each year because of the anticipation of going to the beach and enjoying the opportunity to ride stable horses. I was on the back of a horse every chance I got. My love of these majestic animals was an incredibly passionate drive. I used to ride with my favorite cousin, both at the White Sands Club and later at the Chesapeake Country Club. We had many memorable adventures on the backs of the majestic animals.

When I was ten years old I went riding with some friends of my oldest brother. He told them to protect me. The ride through the bridal paths was beautifully delightful and uneventful. When we came to the main road leading to the stables, they wanted to race. I carefully restrained my horse, wanting to walk slowly. All at once a horse fly bit my leg and instinctively I swatted it. When I did, the reins were relaxed and that was all my horse needed. She was the lead horse and didn't want to be left behind. I was off balance and precariously bouncing in the saddle. She was an enormous horse and I was a petite munchkin. Trying to secure myself in the saddle was impossible and my left ankle slipped through the stirrup and I was sliding down and looking at the horse's hooves. I had a death grip on the saddle horn, but my grip was weak and I knew I was going to die. I began to pray my Act of Contrition as my fingers were losing their grip on the horn. The memory and the visual of those moments remain quite vivid to this day.

All at once I heard the thunder of approaching horses' hooves. My brother's friends caught my horse and my life was spared. I didn't dare tell my mother what had happened since that would have ended my equestrian pursuits. I believe there was an angel helping me to maintain my grip on that saddle horn, and the timing involved in my rescue was nothing short of miraculous. One day I will be face to face with that angel and be able to verbalize my gratitude.

The hand of God was also apparent as I remember a harrowing ride on a Pennsylvania mountain road when I was five years old. All seven of us were in the car. We were on our way to visit relatives who lived in Gallitzin, my mom's home town. My dad was quite a conservative driver who in years past would walk through deep snow to the coal mines rather than drive his car. He always obeyed the speed limit. His only infraction was probably driving too slowly.

As we were ascending a steep mountain road, we were driving at a snail's pace. A huge tractor trailer was in front of us with a heavy load.

My dad saw his chance to pass the big rig on the steep ascent. The left lane was clear. As we got to the front of the rig attempting to complete the pass, we realized that there was another one directly in front of it. As if those weren't enough drama, another large rig was barreling toward us in the left lane. There was no escape because of a steep gorge to our right and large mountain to our left. You could have heard a pin drop in the car. The silence was only surpassed by seven pounding heartbeats and silent screams. At the last minute the tractor decelerated allowing us to squeeze in front of him and we were all saved from certain death.

My young heart knew that we had angels around us and that our lives were spared for a purpose.

The panic of those moments also remains a vivid memory to this day. It was a harbinger of danger and deliverance yet to come.

❧ Journaling ❦

1. *Record any incidences when your life was in danger and yet spared.*

2. *Do you believe it was just luck or do you believe that you were spared for a purpose?*

3. *Are you afraid of danger? When? Where? How?*

4. *What do you do with these fears?*

MIRACLE IN HIGH SCHOOL

Does the Lord truly have a plan for our lives? Does he work all things together for our good? I learned the answer to those questions in a uniquely dangerous way in high school.

I was in my junior year of high school. Since my school was a wonderful private boarding school for girls who would be entering the convent after graduation, the student body was small, friendly, warm, enthusiastic and devoted to the spiritual life. We were a family with an identical purpose, a divine calling. I was delighted and excited to have my life mapped out before me. I wanted to share the love of Jesus Christ with the world.

The Asian flu was particularly bad that year and many people in the country were dying from the ravages of the flu. It raged through our school of 120 young girls. Forty of us were in bed. I remember being in bed for ten days. I valiantly struggled to be strong and not complain.

By divine design, at the end of ten days I needed to return to my home in southern Maryland to get some new glasses. My mother was concerned over my health as I was very weak and dragging my left leg. Filled with stubborn apprehension, both my dad and I refused to consult a doctor about my lethargy.

I returned to school and I remember being reprimanded by the principal and several classmates for trying to get attention by walking so slow. I was exhausted and weak. I had no comprehension of just how ill I was. I refused to listen to my body, pushing myself as hard as I could.

God's grace was all over me. By his awesome provision, the glasses were too strong a prescription and I needed to return home the next weekend to have them checked. This time my mother was not going to take no for an answer. My sister-in-law worked for a doctor and thanks to her influence, I found myself in a doctor's office at midnight. This doctor had two sisters who were Franciscan nuns and he had a particular interest in diagnosing my medical condition.

He ran many tests and concluded that I had miraculously survived encephalitis. I needed to remain home for the next six weeks recuperating and taking medication to help rebuild my immune system. Gradually I regained my strength and was able to return to school. For the next year, I required mega-doses of iron and B vitamins to regain my strength. My main regret at the time was that I missed the national Latin exam. However I was able to take it again my senior year and received Magna Cum Laude on the national scoring system. Despite encephalitis, the Lord had his wonderful hand on my life and protected my brain. He taught my young heart that he cares about every detail of my life and that I can fully trust him.

"For I know the plans I have for you, says the Lord. They are plans for good and not for evil, to give you a future and a hope."

(Jer. 29:11)

❧ JOURNALING ❧

1. *Have you been physically ill and near death?*

2. *Record the events and the results.*

3. *Are you angry with God for any lasting effects? Physical pain?*

4. *Has this limited your choices in life?*

OCEAN CITY ANGEL

T he summer of 1963 I was experiencing the normal joy of summer with no books, tests, or exams, and I was especially thrilled and full of anticipation since I would be experiencing my very first trip to Ocean City, Maryland. Teenage excitement reigned supreme with the crescendo of girlish giggles. The weather was perfectly suited for such a special outing, with the ocean waves beckoning all who would dare to enter its delightful whirlpool of wonder.

My brother and his wife had driven my best friend and me to our day at the beach. We body surfed. We walked the boardwalk, enjoying the arcades, determined to win the largest stuffed bear in the universe. We ate, inhaling boardwalk fries and burgers, all the while interrupting our attempts to swallow with uncontrollable laughter. With our hunger satiated and our confidence overflowing, we returned to the beach.

Seeing the ocean for the first time was an exhilarating adventure only to be surpassed by my novice attempts at body surfing. The waves enchanted me and at times I found myself dizzy from the churning foam. I remember thinking that this was the largest bubble bath ever.

I also remember standing in the surf, waist deep, when I was hit by a huge wave and forced under the waters in a sitting position. I was being dragged and desperately attempted to regain my footing. I was asthmatic, though I did not know it at the time. I recall the panic of having no air left and praying for help, knowing that I was about to die.

All at once, my body seemed to slam with great force against the legs of a young man who pulled me up and out of the water by my hair. As I spotted my friends and began to approach them, everyone in the water seemed near, yet the man was nowhere.

I knew that in a moment, my life had been dramatically spared, saved by a very strong stranger.

I frequently say out loud, "thank you" to the Lord's angels whom have been given charge over me and have rescued me all these years.

Was this stranger an angel? My guess is yes.

"For he will command his angels concerning you to guard you in all your ways."

(Ps. 91:11)

❧ JOURNALING ❧

1. *Do you believe in angels?*

2. *Do you believe your life has been spared due to the presence of angels? Explain.*

TOPPLING TREE

T he year after Mike and I received the Lord, we were praying our evening prayers one February evening. Mike was concerned about a sixty foot pine tree in the back of our lot. The ground was saturated due to a significant amount of melting snow. I was concerned about the possibility of a leak in our basement. Our first Christmas in the house, we awoke to find our rugs, furniture and Christmas presents soaked, including a twelve string guitar. The cleanup took hours of bailing and pumping. We consequently installed a sump pump which remedied the situation as long as the pump was not blocked by debris or a power failure.

When we awoke the following morning, we had been spared from catastrophe. I had washed my hair and was sitting under the hair dryer, a process that always took at least sixty minutes. I was praying and thanking the Lord that our security was in him and not in circumstances. I was thanking him that our fears had been relieved and all was well.

That's when I heard what sounded like a terrible explosion. I jumped, hitting my head, plastic curlers and all, against the top of the hair dryer. I was certain that our heater had exploded, or that a jet from Andrews Air Force Base had crashed. I had witnessed a crash when I was a child in our small town of Morningside, not far from our current home.

The possibility also existed that there had been another bad accident in front of our house. We lived on a treacherous curve and we had experienced five crashes in front of our home.

As I quickly entered the kitchen, I looked out the window over the sink and my questions had been shockingly answered. There, resting on our house, was the sixty foot pine tree! Immediately, I began to call our two dogs. With no response, I went out the sliding glass door and called again. Our small dog, Kappy, was cowering in the back of the lot. Our huge Alaskan malamute was unharmed, asleep under the kitchen window. Needless to say, she was a sound sleeper.

I called Mike and he was able to return home and we enlisted help from neighbors to remove the tree. Much to our surprise and delight, the tree had been caught by the only other tree outside of the kitchen, an old hickory nut tree which eventually died from the shock of the impact. In the entire incident, the only house damage was to one shingle which was sliced by the chain saw!

Did the Lord hear our prayers? I believe the answer is evident. It was quite a visual lesson for us in how much the Heavenly Father cares for and protects us. For me, it was also a learning experience in trusting my husband's concerns, outlook and prayers.

I Peter 5:7 says, *"Cast all your anxiety on him because he cares for you."* The Greek verb used for the word 'cast' is *epiripto*. It is also used when Jesus was entering Jerusalem on Palm Sunday and the disciples cast cloaks on the donkey that he would ride. I love this picture of casting my cares under the authority of Jesus. Just as the unbroken colt submitted to the authority of Jesus, so my anxieties are subject to his authority, if I just cast them on him.

This experience was a 3D visual of how to apply this verse. It was one that we would never forget and would need in the future.

❧ JOURNALING ❧

1. *Do you struggle with anxiety?*

2. *How do you handle this?*

3. *Have you had a good medical check-up?*

4. *Do you pray over anxieties?*

5. *Do you believe that the Lord cares about the events of your life? List specifics.*

Delivered from Fire

Have you ever had one of those intense days when you are almost home and the recliner seems to be beckoning you? You visualize the relaxation. You almost taste the sweet tea. Your toes imagine the relief of elevated feet. I have been there.

The sun was setting as I returned home from a day of fasting and Bible study in Annandale, Virginia. One of my memory verses for the day was from *II Peter 2:12*. *"That day will bring about the destruction of the heavens by force and the elements will melt in the heat."*

As I was pulling in the driveway, my husband was standing in the doorway frantically motioning for me to back out of the driveway quickly. I noticed that the storm door was covered with steam.

Our furnace was a hot water boiler and when my husband arrived home the house temperature was about 90 degrees. He ran to the furnace room to rescue our two Alaskan malamutes. As he entered the room, our furnace which was green, was glowing red, with parts of it exploding like launched missiles around the dogs. Mike hit an emergency cut off switch and brought the dogs up to safety. He called the fire department from our kitchen which was located directly above the furnace room. These were pre-cell phone days.

I remembered the feeling of total helplessness and panic as we stood outside in the darkness. The fire truck was in the neighborhood, but could not find our house. I remember running breathlessly in the streets, waving my arms to no avail. The minutes seemed like an eternity. Our houses were fueled by gas heat and I realized that the entire street could explode at any moment. Several weeks prior to this event, a school house in the west exploded as the boiler launched through the roof like a rocket. Minutes seemed like an eternity as we waited for the fire engine to find us. I wanted to cry, scream and create some kind of a scene that would cause the men to find us. Exhausted with fright I stood still, frozen in place, and finally prayed angelic protection around all of us in the neighborhood.

Having finally found our home, I remember the courage of the young firemen who raced into our house and into the boiler room. They were such young heroes, risking their lives for us! As my heart pounded relentlessly, my maternal instincts engaged and I wanted to hold them back from the threatening danger. They were so brave. They were sons, husbands and fathers.

I stood there powerless, yet confidently praying over our home, our neighbors and these virile rescuers who entered a possible inferno. I was quite aware of total dependence on the Lord's providence.

When the fireman exited our home, they were covered in perspiration and were ashen, stating that the experience had been a 'close one.'

The previous week we had called the gas company as we were smelling gas in our front lawn. As the gas company finished checking out our home, a mistake was made, and they failed to activate an important switch, necessary to keep everything fully operational. By God's amazing grace, no elements melted with intense heat, except for our furnace. God showered us with more grace and we were able to acquire a new furnace. Our home was on the market and had just been sold, so the new owner received a new $5,000 furnace. Our insurance company also paid for us to stay several days in a hotel while the walls of our house were cleaned.

Needless to say, those memory verses have been imprinted on my mind and soul on that memorable day and I praise the Lord for his steadfast protection of our lives all these years. I have been challenged to walk in faith and not fear, remembering that the Lord is in control of every detail of my life.

❧ Journaling ✖

1. *Do you have fears for your personal safety in your home?*

2. *Have you ever experienced irrational fears concerning your safety in your home?*

3. *Do you have practical aids such as a fire detector and a fire extinguisher?*

4. *Do you pray over your safety in your home?*

5. *Do you trust the Lord for your safety?*

ROOT CANAL TERROR

After the incident with the furnace, we sold the house and moved to a contemporary rancher in Upper Marlboro, Maryland. The second year there, I began to experience terribly inexplicable pain in my teeth. Just simple air hitting them was excruciating. It reminded me of my childhood days with cotton balls drenched in Jiffy toothache medicine that we would put in our mouths, filling the cavities. Our dad couldn't afford to take us to the dentist, and mistakenly believed that our permanent molars would fall out like our baby teeth as we aged. That belief, combined with no fluoride in the water, spelled deadly decay.

Confounded by my pain, my dentist gave me a shot of Novocain before dealing with the tooth. It didn't work. So he gave me a second shot. It didn't work. He apologized, explaining that he would have to give me a mandibular block in the back of my mouth. It didn't work. So finally he explained that he would have to open the tooth and shoot the medicine right into the nerve. Finally, it worked. By this time, my mouth was slightly distorted, lips and tongue numb, and thankfully, so also was the problem tooth. He performed the first stage of a root canal on the tooth. It would have to be completed in two weeks when the nerve was dead.

The following day, the very next tooth did the same thing! So I found myself in the dentist's chair again. This time, it only took one injection to numb the tooth.

In a two year period, I would have experienced eleven root canals. When the pain returned to the original tooth, I knew it was time for another opinion. I had been with this dentist for fifteen years and had trusted him implicitly, but there was obviously something wrong that was beyond his ability to diagnose or treat.

I consulted with several specialists and they agreed that I was being incorrectly diagnosed and had received unnecessary root canals. But at this point, they agreed that the teeth would probably need to be crowned for strength. They also agreed that the root canals had been shoddily performed.

My dentist had performed several of them on vital teeth with no Novocain. Prior to doing them, he would place a gel on the tooth and then deliver an electric shock to see if the root was alive. My response to being shocked left no doubt as to the viability of the nerve. These procedures were terribly painful and I was only able to endure them through prayer and slow breathing.

However, having had my mouth open for such long periods of time only exacerbated the underlying and undiagnosed problem. It also precipitated other muscular-skeletal problems.

This led me on a medical quest for answers. I refused to live like this and wanted to be in the hands of competent doctors.

❧ JOURNALING ❧

1. *Do you blindly trust those in authority?*

2. *If betrayed by an authority figure, are you able to trust again?*

3. *Have you sought help if you are having difficulty in trusting?*

4. *Have you found a good counselor?*

5. *Have you given up?*

HUMAN TEST DUMMY

I n the mid '80s I had persevered for five years with my team of doctors, who were attempting to unravel this medical mystery that had been overwhelming my life. During this time our only son, Matthew James Clark, was conceived. His conception and birth were two quite-delightful rainbows in the midst of multiple medical tornadoes.

On August 10, 1990, I was on my way to physical therapy. I was determined to conquer my fears of driving the beltway in heavy rain. The traffic only moved about fifty miles per hour in the fast lane. I managed to stay in the slowest lane. As I arrived at my exit I breathed a sigh of relief. At this point, I was traveling about twenty-five mph and was entering a blind curve when the light turned yellow. I applied my brakes and my Thunderbird began to slide sideways. I remember calmly saying to myself, "OK Margo, get control." The next moment there was the crunching sound of an impact and I remember thinking that someone had hit me. My next conscious thought was two hundred yards later when I awoke with my car in a nauseating spin, ready to go airborne. I screamed, "Lord, save me!" I heard a soft voice saying, "Take your foot off." Instinctively, I pulled both feet up and regained control of the car. I had zigzagged across the medium strip, taking down signs while traveling unconsciously through an intersection, only to be saved short of a major intersection at noon time. My car had collided with another car. My body had sustained great soft tissue damage with every rib dislocated by the seat belt. My jaw was dislocated, my left hip sustained an injury called a pelvic sheer and my left foot was damaged. I had also incurred whiplash which caused miserable migraines to again become a constant companion. Consequently, the previous five years of therapy had been reversed, leaving me in a prison of pain.

One month later in a newly repaired car and on the way to my osteopath for therapy, Matt and I were rear ended by a dump truck while sitting at a stop light. The driver had managed to stop short of crushing us. The truck was sideways, facing the ditch. I drove into the adjacent gas station because I didn't know who else might have been involved. I got out of my car to cautiously approach the driver of the truck. Several moments earlier when I pulled on to the highway, I observed the dump truck about one mile away. I knew it was safe to pull out and go one quarter of a mile for my left turn. After the impact, the driver of the dump truck straightened out his truck and continued driving. I tried to flag him down, but to no avail, since I was on foot and injured. I then drove my son and myself to the doctor and both of us had dislocated pelvises, requiring chiropractic adjustments.

As I continued my journey of healing I refused to give up, or get bitter. I had too much to live for. I held on to the fact that the Lord had an awesome plan for my life.

Fifteen months later my son and I met a similar fate on the 14th Street Bridge in Washington, D.C. While we were sitting in traffic, we were again rear ended by a taxi cab! The phrase Déjà vu was echoing through my bruised brain.

Much to my dismay, I found myself back to square one again and unable to walk by that evening. Thankfully, Matt was not injured since he was secured in his car seat.

During the next two years, I found myself embroiled in ruthless litigation with the cab company. Six lawyers had refused to take my case, as they thought it would be impossible to win with my previous injuries. Adding to the quagmire was the confusion of ownership of the location. Was the accident in the District of Columbia or Virginia? Pursuing the law suit unfortunately exasperated the migraines and the additional stress caused my hair to fall out by the hands full.

In June of 1992, my best friend invited Matt and me to her condo in Ocean City. I was in dire need of a vacation. The second day there, I became very sick and drove myself to the local medical clinic on Ocean Highway while my friend watched our children. I was diagnosed with viral pneumonia. My fever was 104. This was all complicated by undiagnosed asthma. My immune system was seriously compromised due to cumulative stress. In the next eleven months, I would suffer with asthmatic bronchitis seven separate times and also with three cases of strep throat. My body was in a deep, downward spiral.

In May of 1995, I attended a local healing service. During the service I received a dramatic healing of the cervical damage in my neck. The evidence included the facts that the tremor in my right hand and arm instantly disappeared. My migraines were also gone! What a tender touch from the Lord this was. I felt like Alice in Wonderland and Cinderella wrapped up in one! I kept looking in the mirror and giggling with glee at the new me.

One month later my family drove into Washington, D.C. to retrieve some lost relatives from Connecticut. They were quite relieved to be safe and heading to our home for a wonderful vacation. We were sitting at the stoplight on South Capitol Street with the Capitol directly behind us. I was smiling at my future sister-in-law as she sat beside me in the passenger seat. That's when the living nightmare happened again!

A doctor fell asleep at the wheel of his Lexus and struck us so forcefully that I slammed into my brother-in-law's car in front of me, totaling it. He in turn hit the van in front of him. I was wondering why I had to lock my arms and was being violently thrust toward the steering wheel while my future sister-in-law to my right remained secured in her seat by the seatbelt. After all, this was brand new bright blue Neon with multiple safety features. As my mind raced, the doctor panicked, hit the gas, striking my car again. I was struck so forcefully that the seat was broken. It had come off the track, allowing me to be thrust forward like a Raggedy Ann doll. My mind, heart and emotions were attempting to grasp this surreal and tragic accident. Though it happened quickly, I seemed to be experiencing it in slow-motion. The crushing reality raced over my entire being once all the motion stopped. Then the monstrous companion known as pain made the reality of its presence undeniable.

When I instinctively locked my arms upon impact, I caused further damage to my body. I sustained mid back injuries and many of the same injuries incurred in the previous accidents. I was sure that my neck was broken since my entire right arm was numb. I was literally injured from head to toe and taken to a local hospital while Mike, who had been in the car in front of me that I hit, took our relatives home, driving the Neon. My brother-in-law drove his car with his children. Mike didn't know which hospital they were taking me to. The EMT in the ambulance with me was excellent at calming me down. I have often thought of him as an angel of protection. He suggested that I request being transferred to a hospital outside of the city. When the ambulance door was opened, a car raced to the entrance of the ER, blocking any attempts of the EMTs from getting me into the hospital. A woman was screaming hysterically that her husband had been shot. At this point, I felt as though my blood pressure was out of control.

By God's grace, all went well, even when I was having an asthma attack and being totally ignored in the hall of the ER because of those coming in with gunshot wounds. The Lord had his hand on me. Mike did find me eventually and I was released because again, I had been diagnosed with soft tissue injuries.

Hind sight is 100%. I actually had sustained herniated discs in several of the accidents and should have demanded an MRI before being released. Regardless, we were not ready to get involved in litigation again. That was a nightmare that I was unwilling to endure.

The first Sunday after the accident, Mike and I attended church. I hobbled into the sanctuary on crutches. Our senior pastor anointed me with oil. I told him that I absolutely could not stop shaking inside. As he prayed for me, he asked the Prince of Peace to calm me. Immediately, I experienced a wonderful peace that engulfed my entire being. The trembling was totally removed and I received a new insight into what the Prince of Peace could do for me.

For the next seventeen months I was a professional patient who was wondering if she really was a "human test dummy." Once again my life had become a shadow boxing tournament with my dreaded phantom-like enemy known as pain.

In June of 1995, an old friend introduced me to some wonderful supplements containing Chinese herbs. These products quickly helped my body to heal. I lost thirty pounds and experienced exuberant energy. My migraine headaches were also gone. I believed I had a new lease on life. There was light at the end of the tunnel and it wasn't an oncoming train!

In total, I have been in twelve collisions and injured in each one. I have been blessed with wonderful doctors and friends and a husband who refuses to give up on me. He encourages my faith, bolsters my hope and causes my love for him to grow and grow. Despite the most recent collision where I was hit by a state truck which totaled Mike's car, he has hung in there with me. It doesn't get much better than that in a marriage. I am blessed. I am blessed indeed.

"I love the Lord, for he hears my voice; he heard my cry for mercy. Because he turned his ear to me, I will call on him as long as I live. The cords of death entangled me the anguish of the grave came upon me; I was overcome by trouble and sorrow. Then I called on the name of the Lord: 'O Lord, save me!' The Lord is gracious and righteous; our God is full of compassion, The Lord protects the simple hearted; when I was in great need, and he saved me. Be at rest once more, O my soul, for the Lord has been good to you. For you, O Lord, have delivered my soul from death, my eyes from tears, my feet from stumbling, that I may walk before the Lord in the land of the living."

(Ps. 116:1-9)

HEROES

MARGO CLARK

Slow motion battles

Slow motion heroes

Stripped of overdrive,

Stripped of drive.

Experiencing a nauseating, neutral gear,

Watching life proceed in the fast lane.

This new, harassing, depressing battle,

Harbingers new victories,

Gained in slow motion,

Through a New, Abiding, Resurrection Power and Presence.

Purple Hearts,

Silver and

Bronze Medals

For Perseverance,

Character

And Triumphing Love.

❧ Journaling ❧

1. *Have you ever felt forsaken by God?*

2. *Have you ever had close friends accuse you of doing something wrong that might have been the cause of the trouble?*

3. *Did you ever believe what was happening was punishment from the Lord?*

4. *Have you ever prayed to die?*

5. *What did you do to get help?*

6. *Do you believe that there could be a rainbow in your present tornado?*

A DREAM HUG

I n 1985 I was again sitting in a doctor's office, overwhelmed with pain. I had seen seventeen medical specialists and not one doctor had an answer for what I was enduring. I had decided to hire three of the seventeen to unravel the mystery contained in this enigmatic labyrinth of confusing agony.

My first choice was a TMJ specialist who believed that he knew the answers. As I waited for him, my neck was severely aggravated by a pinched nerve affecting every nerve ending in my neck and head. He decided that my jaw was quite crooked from years of grinding my teeth while sleeping. He made me an acrylic appliance that needed to be adjusted weekly.

That evening, as I settled down attempting to enter the surrender of sleep, I eventually dreamed about being in a dentist's chair. A doctor whom I had never seen came to me and asked me if I wanted to be held. He had very kind eyes and exuded a warm confidence. I said yes. As he embraced me, I became like a little infant. *Deut. 33:12* states *"Let the beloved of the Lord rest secure in him, for he shields him all day long, and the one the Lord loves rests between his shoulders."*

I remember releasing an incomprehensible weight as I sank into his shoulder, the weight of a megaton bomb just kept sinking deeper and deeper into his shoulder. He said my head needed to be x-rayed. He held me during the set of circular x-rays.

All at once we were walking through the green grassy field behind the house where I grew up. He was holding my hand and told me that everything was going to be alright. He told me that I had five skull fractures, but that I would heal. Actually the field was level, but in this dream, it just gently ascended as I walked with him holding my hand. I remember walking higher and higher in the field with him and then the dream ended. I remember waking up and I was crying uncontrollably.

We had rarely been held as children due to my mother's shriveled right arm. My dad creatively engineered a contraption to hold our bottles in the cribs. My father was abusive when he drank and I never remembered a safe hug or being able to relax near him.

This was more than a 3D dream. It was my heavenly Father, restoring the years that the locusts had eaten (Joel 2:23) and loving a little child inside of this grown woman's body.

I prayed never to forget that hug. Throughout the years, the dream has lost some of its vivid awareness, but the memory of the weight coming out of my body is still quite a tangible memory. As a result of the dream, I have been left with knowledge of being loved by my heavenly Father, and an awareness that a wonderful day will come when I will experience that hug for eternity.

❧ JOURNALING ❧

1. *Have you ever had a vivid dream that you knew was a gift from the Lord?*

2. *What did you receive from it?*

BULLET HOLE

I n the fall of 1987, I was sitting in our living room nursing our new baby boy. We had endured seventeen years of infertility and the Lord blessed us with a healthy son. Needless to say, I was quite protective. I was one of those new moms who was sure that the doctor was going to drop my baby right after delivery. This fear was heightened when I was not allowed to hold him for almost two days. He was being observed for a possible heart problem. Once he was in my arms, I never wanted to put him down or have anyone else hold him.

While I was relaxing on our couch, enjoying our new bundle of joy, I heard an unusual 'pinging' sound. I jumped up and instinctively covered his head and turned him away from the window.

There was a bullet hole in our front window, just a few feet from where we were sitting! The Lord's hand was surely protecting us. The bullet penetrated the storm window and did not penetrate the main window. To this day, we have not repaired or replaced that storm window. Each time I look at it, I am reminded that we are surrounded by the Lord's angels who have been given charge over us. It is an incredible faith builder.

Not only did the Lord protect our son in the womb, but also in my arms from the machinations of the evil one.

Truly we worship the living God whose purposes will not be thwarted.

"Let the beloved of the Lord rest securely in him, for he shields him all day long, and the one the Lord loves rests between his shoulders."

(Deut. 33:13)

55

❧ Journaling ❧

1. *Do you know that you are loved by the Lord?*

2. *Can you think of a time when you were protected by him?*

3. *Do you rest between his shoulders, which means over his heart?*

4. *If you are not sure, pray and ask the Father to show you his love for you.*

ONE STEP FORWARD, TEN STEPS BACK

I n 1983 as I proceeded with the therapy for my jaw, a fire-storm of perplexing pain dominated every waking moment. Migraines had become a constant companion. In addition, I found myself screaming aloud as the sensation of seven to eight knives piercing my back doubled me over. Once the attack had passed, I found that for the next three days I was unable to sit up without falling forward. I didn't seem to have the strength to hold my back erect. I also discovered that I couldn't hold the steering wheel for more than five seconds before having to change hands while driving to the doctor. This necessitated our purchasing a new car for me that had every electric convenience.

Doctor after doctor had no explanation for what was happening to my body. As usual, when they had no explanation, the answer had to be psychological. So I went to see a psychiatrist in the Bethesda area of the Washington suburbs. I had blood work done and my TMJ specialist was sure that it was all a chemical imbalance. The blood work was normal so there was no chemical imbalance. I took a test that had 700 questions. This would give a psychological profile. I wrote as fast as I could since my arms didn't want to work, and I had trouble sitting up. A dear friend had driven me. The doctor had declared me quite sane.

I remember thinking that I was dying of some rare form of MS. I definitely was losing the ability to control my muscular-skeletal system. I was also losing confidence in the diagnostic skills of specialists. I spent more and more time in bed. I had made up my mind that I was not going to become bitter and that I would keep praising and thanking the Lord despite all that was happening. I reasoned that if I couldn't sit up, I could still rest on the bed and read, except, I lost the ability to hold a book. So I determined that I would put my small cassette tape recorder beside me in bed and listen to the Bible. That only worked for a short span of time, because the migraines were so out of control that any sound was agonizing.

I remember feeling like I was in a tomb. I asked myself what would King David do in my shoes and remembered that he was quite honest with the Lord. So I looked at the ceiling and with a very loud voice said, "I am being slain." I heard a gentle voice in my spirit who said, "Yes, you are." I was terrified. I reasoned that the Lord could leave me like this for years to come and it was alright because he was holy, righteous and just.

For the next several months, I remembered breathing only shallow breaths. This former nun could do nothing to win brownie points with the Lord. Even though I understood the gospel message and the free gift of grace, at a very deep level, the Lord was dealing with my need to earn approval. Was he pleased with me when I was a mess and unable to be productive using my gifts and talents? This frightening question haunted me, stealing the breath from the depths of my diaphragm.

Then the Lord began to whisper Psalm 23 to me, week by week, verse by verse, and my fears gradually began to melt away. I knew he was going to heal me but I didn't want to do what he was telling me to do.

I loved my rose colored glasses and my people pleasing temperament, but the Lord told me that he wanted me to be a Deborah, who was a Biblical Judge, and Prophetess, and a leader. I did get out of that bed and obey the Lord. I continued with the doctors and began to experience healing.

It seems that I had a severe case of TMJ, combined with fibromyalgia and myofascial pain. I had these things before the medical community even identified them. Eventually a neurologist explained to me that I had been having unusually severe trigger point attacks in my back muscles that were so violent that they sprained my back and neck. That is why I couldn't sit up for several days after the attacks. At least that was another confirmation that I was still sane despite the pain.

The body work that I was having done was overwhelmingly painful. The doctor had to break up the locked muscle tissues which were like cement. After he began working on me, I began to recover and the combination of the three therapies was exactly what I needed. Unfortunately, only my osteopath was covered by insurance, but I had to pay everything in advance and file my own claims. Consequently our finances were stressed to the maximum which added to the overall stress.

But the Lord saw us through. At one point a fabulous relative wrote us a generous check, keeping us afloat.

Our God is faithful and delivered us from the enemy's attacks. How could we not love this God and praise him with every breath?

❧ JOURNALING ⚜

1. *Have you ever been involved in an unrelenting crisis in which you felt hopeless, abandoned, and judged?*

2. *How did you react?*

3. *Have you found resolution to your predicament?*

4. *How has this affected your faith and your hope?*

5. *Do you still trust God's plan for your life?*

CAPTAIN HOOK

The birth of our son Matthew was a refreshing oasis in the midst of a medical nightmare. Raising him was a new experience for Mike and me, and I prayed daily that I would not warp him through the unintended mistakes of ignorance.

Danger is present in many forms, real and imaginary, in the eyes and minds of our children. Fantasy and reality frequently blur. Consequently we proactively protect our children, parenting them through their fears, assuring them that there are no monsters under the bed.

There are those moments in every Mother's memory that she records so that they will not be forgotten. One of these moments remains forever part of Mike and my heart's treasured memories. It was the year of Captain Hook.

The world of Captain Hook, as personified by Dustin Hoffman in the movie, *Hook*, swirled in our little son's imagination. The movie had been a family favorite. It was the time when our recreation room was a littered landscape of Playmobile toys, and our home was the house of choice for the neighborhood boys. Rifles, pistols and swords were brandished on both levels of our home and occasionally became unsightly and precarious lawn ornaments. In the spring and summer seasons, they were buried in their shallow graves only to become entangled in the summer's lawn mower blades. In the autumn season it was not unusual to rake up a child's weapon of choice in the swirling mound of leaves.

Our recreation room was a land of imaginative wonder. One such land was the Frontier Fort, a spacious arena of soldiers, guns and horses.

Mysteriously one play day all of the soldiers' hats disappeared never to be recovered. (No soldier perished as a result of this mishap!)

There were frontier towns, wagon trains, farms with innumerable animals, a tropical island and two enormous castles. Many a delightful trip had been made to the toy stores seeking an entire collection. There were afternoons that I believed my calling in life was to protect Maid Marian from Robin Hood and his band of unruly men.

All of these play lands had many small people and all the trappings of their particular historical era. It would remind me of my childhood and the trunk I had for my dolls, except multiplied by hundreds. All these tiny toys required quite a bit of work to keep organized. In those years I learned the peculiar form of play used by the male species. After meticulous care and hours of setting up the scenes, my son and his friends would love to totally destroy any semblance of order. The recreation room looked like a tornado had carved its devastating path in seconds. My husband would comfort me and assure me that this behavior was known as 'boy.'

It was during one of these seasons when my son was four that he had prayed with my husband to accept the Lord Jesus Christ as his personal Savior. It was such a precious time in his life as he comprehended the realities of Heaven and Hell. My husband is a pastor and we had been one of five couples that started a church in southern Maryland. Our son was involved in seeing a church be birthed and grow because of the Lord's blessings.

The year prior to his spiritual birth, one memorable afternoon, he had been playing with his Playmobile Pirate Ship in his bedroom. Pirates climbed high, clinging to the masts as great storms gusted through his room. Canons stood ready to protect all pirates and their treasures from other pillagers of the high seas. This was very serious play and my son's face registered highly focused emotions. At times his little voice would become deep as he entered the world of pirates. He was on his knees organizing his men for what was sure to be a grand battle when his face became quite serious. He seemed unusually upset and asked me if Captain Hook was a good man or a bad man. I paused, not sure of how to wisely answer this significant question. I finally told him that I thought he was a bad man. My son shrieked with the horror of disbelief screaming, "why?" Knowing that I had given the wrong answer, I prayed for wisdom and internal calm and said that perhaps no one had told him about Jesus' love for him. His face registered great relief and a smile covered his countenance. Somehow I knew a great storm had just passed and for a moment, I had been in the center of it with my son. I sighed and walked away only to hear whimsical whispering coming from my son's room. I peeked around the corner and saw him picking up each pirate tenderly informing each one, "Pirate, Jesus loves you." I walked away with my heart dancing.

In the middle of imaginary cannon fire and swashbuckling, the only fear gripping my son was that of Captain Hook's eternal destiny.

My husband and I shared this memory together that evening, wondering if any other child on planet earth was fretting over the salvation of Captain Hook and his men?

❧ JOURNALING ❧

1. *Have you experienced intense trepidation at the thought of raising a new born infant?*

2. *How did you handle your fears?*

3. *Where did you go in your quest for wisdom and knowledge?*

4. *What advice would you give a new parent struggling with apprehension?*

MIRACLE AT McDONALD'S

The elation of our son's concern for Captain Hook and his men was soon traumatically tempered one afternoon. It was a lazy spring day and I was returning from an all day excursion in southern Maryland, which was about thirty minutes driving time from our home. I approached the little strip mall one mile from our housing development. There are two traffic lights within a quarter mile on that particular strip of RT 301 in Maryland. The first traffic light had turned yellow as I entered the intersection, and I could see the light ahead of me turning red. I was driving a small bright blue Neon. As I slowed for the traffic light, I was looking at our miniscule McDonald's, perhaps one of the smallest in the country, and then I heard the terrifying sound of screeching tires close to me. As I looked in my rear-view mirror, I saw a gargantuan tractor trailer careening toward my bumper, burning rubber as he skidded. There was a narrow breakdown lane to my right with a steep incline leading to the McDonald's and the shopping center.

I was shocked that the big rig had decided to run the light, since the light was clearly red and visible from the previous light. I screamed out in prayer and much to my amazement, the vehicle had managed to stay upright in the breakdown lane beside me. At that moment, when the smoke cleared, I saw a second tractor trailer coming toward my little Neon. The other traffic was already crossing in front of me preparing to enter the strip mall. I eased my vehicle into the intersection and the second trailer was able to veer to the right, stopping beside me.

Since that sobering moment, I can count eleven times that I have been rear ended, yet by God's amazing provision, I am still vertical and somewhat alert!

One of my friends has told me that when we get to heaven, they will know my angels, because they will be the ones with the crimped wings!

I love God's word and am reminded of *Ps. 91:11*, *"For he will command his angels concerning you to guard you in all your ways: they will lift you up in their hands, so that you will not strike your foot against a stone."* When I see them one day I will enjoy thanking them, face to face.

Are there angels at McDonald's? I believe so.

❧ JOURNALING ❧

1. *Have you ever been in a dangerous situation where you knew your life could possibly end in seconds?*

2. *What did you say, think, or do?*

3. *Do you have any residual nightmares?*

4. *Do you have a plan of action in case of similar danger?*

5. *Are you able to practice being in the presence of the Lord?*

REC ROOM ANGEL

My son's junior year of high school proved to be a year during which his faith would be tried by fire. He was surrounded by wonderful and godly friends both at school and in our church youth group. Deep relationships had been forged that will last a lifetime.

In his church youth group, one of the young ladies had been stricken with cancer. All of the teens prayed and fasted continually. I remember the last night that our son had visited her. He spent the night on his knees expecting a miracle. This awesome young lady had spent her last evening with the youth group praying over each of them. She told them that she knew where she was going, but wanted to make sure that they knew where they would be spending eternity. She had met with our pastor, planning her funeral. She wanted the Lord to be glorified through it all.

The Lord took her home that last evening. Many of the teens were devastated. They had the same nagging question. Did God answer prayer? Followed by, why pray at all? Our son had begun a long faith journey. I remember hours of prayer for our son during this time in his young life.

During this time a favorite worship song was "Oh Praise Him" by the David Crowder Band. Our son had been playing his bass and singing this particular praise song on the stage during a church service when he heard hundreds of angels singing! There were only about thirty-five people at this service. It was a new type of service that we were adding. What he was hearing emphasized the initial words of the song regarding listening to the angels singing their praises to the Lord. He surprised me by buying the CD for my birthday. It remains my favorite praise song. I was beginning to see an answer to our prayers regarding his young faith and our privileged task of persevering in prayer.

Perseverance in prayer was a tangible reality in our household as I was experiencing horrific migraine headaches during these years. The migraines lasted for twenty-three years before some surgery helped relieve the most severe symptoms of occipital neuralgia pain, which was a constant companion whose pressured presence I learned to displace through praise music.

One particular evening, our son was praying before going to bed and he prayed, "Lord, I believe that evil will come against our house this evening. I'm asking for angels to protect us or you yourself if you're not too busy." That particular evening I was experiencing a terrible three day migraine which prevented me from falling asleep. My husband had quickly slipped into a deep sleep and was snoring loudly. I asked our son to pull out the air mattress in our rec room so that I could enjoy silence and hopefully fall asleep. I wrapped my head in ice and curled up in a sleeping bag.

When I nestled in the bag, I saw a sharp light on the wall over my right shoulder. I was aggravated because I thought it was coming from my neighbor's porch light. This seemed like the final straw that would break me during a three day migraine. I closed my eyes, covered my head which was wrapped in ice and cocooned myself deep in the sleeping bag. During the evening, I was awakened to see a glowing figure on the wall. It was about eight feet tall and I was filled with tremendous peace and warmth which flowed through my entire body. Comforted, I drifted off to sleep again. A second time I was awakened to see the same glowing figure over my right shoulder. Again, feeling warmly comforted, I drifted off to sleep. A third time I was awakened to see the figure over my right shoulder. I was filled with an indescribable peace and warmth. Again, I effortlessly surrendered to the gift of an extraordinary slumber.

In the morning my husband came down to the laundry to iron some handkerchiefs. I awakened and scrambled up to the bedroom to curl up under the covers and get some more sleep. I was unable to sleep and realized that the basement room where I had been sleeping was sealed from light. As I grasped what had happened, I ran out to tell my husband, but he had just left for work. I eagerly waited for our son to wake up to share the amazing incident with him. When I told him, he turned ashen, telling me what he had prayed the night before. I told him to go and write it down on the computer because some day in the future one of his children might ask him if God answered prayer. He could tell them about the night the Lord brought the angel in response to his prayers, saving his mother's life. His faith was greatly strengthened that night. The Lord was taking him from an evening of prayer for a friend with cancer to a night of prayer for protection for our family.

I later read the medicinal insert for the migraine prescription and realized that I had experienced a full-blown allergic reaction to the potent medicine. A friend at church who is a nurse told me that when someone is slipping into a coma, the medical staff would keep trying to rouse them. I was roused three times that evening by a heavenly visitor.

One of my favorite verses is *Ps. 34:7*, *"The angel of the Lord encamps around those who fear him and delivers them."* I will remember that warmth of my heavenly visitor and the peace that coursed through, and caressed my body that night. I will remember to persevere in prayer. I rejoice in the warmth of the love of my Lord for our family and his tender nurturing of our son's teenage faith. Don't give up. The Lord hears and answers our prayers in his own timing.

❧ JOURNALING ❧

1. *Have you ever felt like your prayers were not being answered?*

2. *Did you give up?*

3. *Did you eventually see your prayers answered?*

4. *Do you keep a prayer journal?*

PARALYSIS

W hat was this strange tingling and numbness in my hands? Why was I dropping so many things?

My mind was dizzy with medical diagnoses and contradicting opinions from different specialists. All I was sure of was the fact that my chiropractor was usually right. So I drove fifty minutes to his office in southern Maryland.

He took x-rays and told me that he was amazed that I was functioning at all, much less at such a high level, able to teach both piano and guitar to a myriad of students. He showed me the x-ray and told me that I was in danger of being paralyzed. The spinal cord in my neck was close to being severed due to the abundance of arthritis in the area of C-4, C-5 and C-6. He ordered an MRI which I was then going to take with me to several experts for their additional opinions.

The last thing he said to me when I was leaving his office was, "Whatever you do, don't get in another car accident, or you could be paralyzed!"

My mind was spinning as I left his office and the chilling exhortation caused me to increase my prayers for protection. The last thing I wanted was to be in another accident.

Five days later my son and I were returning from school in a heavy rain. Matt drove quite carefully and we took a longer route home for safety, avoiding the dangerous road that we normally traveled. It was treacherous in rain. As we approached our development, Matt patiently waited at the light for the traffic light to signal our forward movement. When we made our left on to the northbound portion of a major highway, it happened! All of a sudden the SUV hydroplaned on the turn, and as Matt corrected, it began to tip. I panicked and screamed, "No, Matt!" My tone caused more panic in both of us. We swerved side to side and all I could hear were my doctor's last words as I saw ravines on both sides of us. I saw myself in a wheelchair for the rest of my life. I had witnessed this happening to the parent of one of my sixth grade students years before.

Thank the Lord! Matt was able to gain control of the vehicle and we both apologized for our reactions during the intense fright. Matt asked me to explain what had happened since he was neither speeding nor being reckless. I explained as best I could and though it gave both of us quite a scare, it also afforded us the opportunity to give thanks and praise for our protection. I believe it was a sobering learning lesson for a young driver who has been quite responsible behind the wheel.

That day, Matt's reactions saved both of our lives.

Were there angels in that intersection with us? I believe so.

❧ JOURNALING ❧

1. *Has your faith grown stronger because your life was spared by angelic intervention?*

2. *Explain.*

3. *Do you believe that the Lord hears and answers the prayers for your children?*

4. *Have you stopped praying for them?*

LILIES

I t was the fall of 2004. The swirling leaves had surrendered their ravenous glory to the inevitable change of seasons, performing their dazzling dance of death to the gentle autumnal breezes, harbingers of the approaching winter's wonder. This is my favorite season of the year since Mike and I fell in love in the autumn of 1969. My heart always seems to beat faster with the glories of this season, present and past.

A mixture of joyous nostalgia and frightening, impending danger filled my emotions since I had finally received a sobering diagnosis explaining the perplexing symptoms of vertigo, pain and nausea that had routinely precipitated unrelenting migraine headaches. My new medical vocabulary had expanded to include the term superior semicircular canal dehiscence. I was missing the superior canal in the inner ear on both sides of my head. Fixing the problem meant an invasive surgery, one that would involve cutting the entire side of my head open, removing bone, and exposing my brain during the four hours of surgery. All the normal risks of surgery would be present. There was a great possibility of heart attack or stroke with this surgery. I would be hospitalized for five days because of the additional risks of hemorrhage and stroke. The surgery was my choice since my diagnosis was not life threatening. I decided to consent to the surgery and hospitalization since living with my symptoms was no longer tolerable, especially for a piano, guitar and keyboard teacher.

In addition to the limitations to my teaching career, I was enduring another disappointing frustration. For six years I had been unable to sing in my normal soprano range without a severe earache in my left ear. This triggered an intense migraine attack which lasted a minimum of three days. The inability to use my voice to sing God's praises was a source of immense vexation. For years I had performed as a soloist.

As I was driving to my chiropractor the week before my surgery, I had decided to sing the David Crowder Band's "Oh Praise Him" and endure the consequences. As I began to sing, I noticed a vendor beside the road to the left of my SUV selling chrysanthemums and pumpkins. Simultaneously, I began to smell lilies, so I looked to the right as I drove and then to the left, looking for another vendor selling lilies. I thought this strange since it was the week before Thanksgiving. The fragrance became stronger and stronger, permeating my vehicle. I began to realize that this was not a natural phenomenon. The words of the song echoed, "How infinite and sweet this love so rescuing. O, how infinitely sweet this great love that has redeemed..."

I began to tremble, realizing this was a supernatural presence. It continued to fragrantly permeate the air as I drove the next nine miles. I began to weep and pray, "I love your love, I love your love." As soon as the praise song ended, the fragrance was gone and I knew this was a kiss from God. I knew that I would be totally enveloped in his presence throughout the upcoming surgery even as I had been engulfed in the fragrance of lilies in the SUV.

During the surgery I was in the operating room for four and one half hours. When the surgeon opened the side of my head, preparing to create the missing canal, he discovered that my mastoid bone was damaged, inordinately filled with gaping holes. He first had to fill the holes with surgeon's cement before proceeding with creating the missing superior canal. After making the repair, he closed the side of my head, sewing and stapling the flap of skin shut. He managed to do this without cutting my hair, a fact for which I was totally grateful. As best I knew how, I had prepared my young students to see me with very short hair on the left side of my head.

The operation had caused me to lose equilibrium. I had to learn to walk again with the aid of a walker in the hospital, followed by a cane once home. Five days after the surgery, I returned home, having spent Thanksgiving Day in intensive care.

I had a series of daily walking exercises to perform in the hallway of our ranch style home. The walls of the corridor provided suitable boundaries in case I lost my balance. I was able to carefully return to my teaching routine within several weeks. Part of my recovery exercises for the next year would include walking through the mall and turning my head from right to left. Initially this left me quite dizzy, but eventually, I regained balance.

The surgery was a total success. I was again able to sing and the nauseating vertigo was alleviated. I was only the third person in my doctor's career to have this surgery. My husband and I were able to pray over my doctor's hands before the surgery and since it was a teaching hospital, we were able to pray over all the doctors, nurses and anesthesiologists before the surgery.

The 'lily of the valley' had dramatically reassured me of his presence, direction and protection. I experienced the peace of God that exceeds our human understanding before, during, and after the surgery. I marvel at the Lord's mercy and loving kindness that removed me from such an intolerable cauldron of suffering, and allowed me to function and joyfully serve him.

It would not be the last time that I smelled the lilies. Many more times, I would be blessed with the wonderful fragrance, all during times of need and of worship.

"For in the day of trouble he will keep me safe in his dwelling; he will hide me in the shelter of his tabernacle and set me high upon a rock. Then my head will be exalted above the enemies who surround me; at his tabernacle will I sacrifice with shouts of joy. I will sing and make music to the Lord."

(Ps. 25:3-6)

❧ JOURNALING ❧

1. *Do you make the Lord your dwelling?*

2. *Are you aware that he will hide you during times of trouble?*

3. *Is there a time when you believe that the Lord did not protect you?*

4. *How has that affected your faith?*

THE FRAGRANCE OF LILIES ONCE AGAIN

T he end of the school year was approaching and the pressures of an upcoming recital were exacerbated one morning by an incredibly slow driver ambling along a narrow, dangerous road that lead to school.

Once at school, I had only five minutes to position my portable keyboard in the worship center before the children entered for chapel. This particular morning, I had filled the car with costumes for the recital and needed to carry them all in the classroom before setting up my keyboard. I had allowed enough time for both my son and me to arrive and unload the vehicle. However, "Sergeant Slow Bro" as my son and I had dubbed him was returning to his home, having purchased his newspaper and coffee from a local country store. My son and I had learned his routine and been able to leave earlier so as to avoid being caught behind his old pickup truck. However this particular morning, much to my dismay, he had changed his routine.

As I was driving, I was totally frantic inside. Let's just say that the words in my head were not exactly those that would glorify the Lord. I also was confessing sin every couple of minutes because of those words. I didn't want to be a bad example to my son. Actually, I was screaming inside and 'help me' was one of my most intense prayers.

As we neared our destination, Sergeant Slow Bro made the turn into his house. The light had turned red and it was probably the longest light in the state or perhaps the country. So in my haste, I decided to make a right on to a major highway and I put the pedal to the metal. I also was confessing sin in this regard. I knew if I went north, waited at the next light, I could go south again and save ninety seconds.

My son and I made it to school, no thanks to my reckless driving, and I began to unload the costumes. My son exhorted me to leave them, but I refused, therefore incurring an asthma attack. I needed to make a second trip. I feared leaving the costumes because we were in a dangerous neighborhood and cars were frequently broken into. We hastily unloaded the costumes and began to take my keyboard and stand into the worship center. We had about three minutes. We needed to go through two sets of heavy doors. As we took several steps, I smelled the fragrance of flowers and thought there might have been a wedding the night before. As we moved, I observed that the stage area had no flowers. I ascertained that they just had to be close to us. It made no sense. That is when I was totally engulfed with the presence of lilies! I stopped my son for a moment as we were between the doors, keyboard in hand, and asked him if he had been praying for me during the drive. He answered no. I then asked him if he could smell the lilies. He again said no. Then I began to cry, overwhelmed with the realization that even in my totally frantic moments when I couldn't pull it together, the Lord had heard my prayers, forgiven my foolishness, protected us and given me a heavenly kiss in the form of fragrant lilies. I told my son what was happening and asked him to forgive me for being so rash and endangering us by speeding.

The realization of such love, mercy and grace opened my eyes in a new way to how much the Lord cares for us. It was not the last time I would smell the lilies. Many times in worship at our church and at special moments, the Lord makes his presence known 'fragrantly.'

❧ JOURNALING ❧

1. *How do you seek the Lord's presence?*

2. *Have you ever been surprised by his presence?*

3. *Do you take time to quiet your heart and be still in his presence?*

4. *Read Ps. 46:10. Pray for the Spirit to quiet the noise inside your soul.*

SOPHOMORIC ASSISTANCE

I t had been quite a long day of teaching. I was traveling home with Matt, a sophomore in high school, and his neighborhood friend. I remember praying for strength as I was enduring an unrelenting migraine and seasonal allergies that were aggravating my asthma and therefore making the day a grueling grind. All I wanted to do was collapse and cry in a dark room. Crying was an unaffordable luxury, since it triggered both asthma attacks and allergies. The trip home from school seemed capricious, punishing me with every red light that became a formidable obstacle, forcing me to wait when waiting didn't seem like an option.

When we finally arrived home, my son and his friend went down to the man cave to play their video game. I went into the master bath and began to cry uncontrollably. Finally, I told myself to stop or I would be in deeper trouble. I stopped crying, or so I thought, and found myself gasping for air. No tears were coming down my face and I realized that I was in a terrible asthma attack.

I ran to the kitchen where the parts of the nebulizer were beside the sink. I had rinsed them out after using the machine in the morning. I quickly brought them over to the machine and began to assemble the unit. My hands were shaking dreadfully and I was starting to black out from hyperventilation and therefore, oxygen deprivation.

All of a sudden my son was at my side holding me up as my knees were buckling, and he began assembling the nebulizer for me. He calmly supported me and encouraged me to take in slow, deep breaths. I felt total panic as I heard the sounds in my chest making a foreboding, rattling noise. Matt remained extremely calm and told me that I was doing a good job. He commented on each breath, telling me how much better each breath sounded. I remember looking up into his face while tears cascaded down my cheeks, and I was able to draw confidence from my son who commented on each breath with the maturity of a skilled EMT. I was reminded of the words from the Christmas song, *Mary Did You Know?* I especially related to the words, 'this child that you delivered would soon deliver you.'

I began to feel a calm confidence. My son was speaking life and breath into his mother. We finished the treatment successfully and all I could do after that was ask him why he came upstairs to check on me since I had not been able to call for help. He told me that he heard me making all kinds of unusual noise in the kitchen. This still confuses me as our kitchen is very small and I was just handling light plastic parts of the nebulizer. The video game they were playing was loud and should have muffled any sound I was making. Much to my surprise, I was impressed that the Lord had alerted my son, giving him years of maturity that exceeded his sophomoric grade.

I witnessed my son conduct himself as a man who could handle life and death stress. Though sophomore means wise fool, I believe my son redefined it that day as 'wise man.'

❧ JOURNALING ❧

1. *Have you prayed over your child or children and wondered if your prayers would see fruition?*

2. *Have you ever felt like giving up on intercession for your children? For your family?*

3. *What encourages you to persevere in intercession?*

TREES AND ANSWERED PRAYER

We were experiencing one of the worst winters in Washington D.C.'s history. Our snowfall that particular winter exceeded all snowfalls of the last century. Gazing out my windows at the dazzling white wonderland that surrounded me, I was overwhelmed at its pristine beauty. I marveled at the fact that no two snowflakes are the same. I found myself reflecting with awe on the infinity of God's creation.

Our back yard extends about twelve feet and then drops dramatically into a ravine. It then ascends to a magical forest of intrigue. There was a giant oak tree that has been home to hundreds of July fireflies. It had been a delight to our eyes for many years. My husband was convinced that it was an historic tree.

Several years ago there was a terrible tornado in Maryland that decimated the town of La Plata, which is located about 30 miles south of us. Initially it was thought to be an F-5. Later it was categorized as an F-4. Regardless of its numerical value, it was a fierce and frightening storm. By God's grace, we were unscathed by the storm. Much prayer covered us during that time. I frequently find myself praying over the trees behind our house since they could easily pulverize our roof if they were to fall on it. We had poignantly learned this lesson in our first home with the deliverance from the falling pine tree.

One Saturday morning, a week after the devastating tornado in Southern Maryland we were all busy with various activities, when there was a terrible crashing sound. The huge oak tree behind our house had split into three sections. One section fell and struck my next door neighbor's house, tearing off the back upper deck. Another section fell directly south into the woods. The third section was precariously listing over our house.

We began to pray over that remaining section. *Psalm 16:5* says, *"You have assigned me my portion and my cup; you have made my lot secure."* During storms, I frequently prayed that portion of Scripture back to the Lord.

We had several tree removal companies come out and give us estimates on cutting down the remaining portion of the tree. Several refused to fell the tree, saying it was too dangerous. Meanwhile, we slept in the front section of the house on air mattresses for eight nights. Finally one company agreed to come and remove the listing tree. In a matter of several minutes it was safely down with a deafening sound.

After much rejoicing, I realized the Lord's provision in this circumstance. There were three of us living in our house. The Lord allowed the tree to split into three sections, none of which harmed us or our neighbor. He had truly made our lot secure.

As I gaze out my back window each day, I see the huge oak tree stretched on the ground in three directions and I am reminded of God's faithfulness, of the Trinity's love. That is the second tree he has brought down, so faithfully answering prayer. I find this visual reminder of God's protection a source of great comfort when I am fear prone.

"The boundary lines have fallen for me in pleasant places."

(Ps. 16:6)

❧ JOURNALING ❧

1. *Do you find it easy to trust the Lord in little things, but difficult to trust him in big things?*

2. *How do you nurture your faith?*

3. *Do you have difficulty trusting the Lord, people, family? Why?*

4. *Have you prayed and asked him to grow your faith and trust?*

5. *Do you have a good comprehension of the difference between safe and dangerous people?*

RODS, SCREWS, AND SNOW FLAKES

S everal years after the tornado we were blanketed in a blinding blizzard. We had three feet of snow covering the neighborhood. Our young neighbor across the street had a snow blower and worked for hours clearing the driveways and sidewalks of multiple neighbors. Mike had gone out to help him and they were a formidable team.

It was one of those Hallmark picture days when everything is pristine white, and hot cider, hot chocolate, fires, and delicious oven roasts all blend together to complement the landscape with the fragrances that delight the olfactory senses. Out of necessity everyone hibernated for several days before the roads were plowed.

I waited multiple days before I dared to drive for supplies. I managed to acquire what I needed for an upcoming piano recital. As I approached my SUV, I carefully negotiated every step. There were mounds of snow in the parking lot obscuring visibility. It was a windy day with thirty-five to forty mile an hour winds. I opened the hatch of the SUV, placing my bags in the back. All at once a gust of wind caught the hatch and it slammed down on my head and back, flattening me in the back of my vehicle with the packages. I knew that I was hurt. I was woozy and unsure of my physical condition. I was able to slowly stand up straight and gingerly got into the vehicle. After several minutes, I decided to drive ten miles farther south to my chiropractor. Upon my arrival it was evident that the office was closed for the day. I was about thirty miles from home and I needed medical attention. I cautiously began the drive home and almost drove farther to the hospital because I needed x-rays, but I felt so weak that I decided to continue travelling toward home.

I iced my head and put moist heat on my neck and shoulders. The impact of the hatch also aggravated migraines. By God's amazing grace, my extremities were working normally. I realized that the previous surgery had protected my neck because the fusion with a rod and eight screws served to hold Humpty Dumpty together. Never did I think that such hardware would protect me from extreme danger. I praised my loving Father for such provision.

The year before, I had been leaving school in a snowstorm. School had been closed early. I was carrying a guitar in my left hand and my books in a case in my right hand. I used the remote to unlock the SUV. I brushed the snow from the back window and opened it. I placed my guitar and books inside and when I closed the hatch, it exploded in my face and glass was everywhere! Trembling and covered with glass and debris, I cleared the glass from my body and also from the SUV, and placed the guitar and books in the vehicle. I was freezing. It was almost impossible to get any heat to be effective in the SUV with no back window to block the snow, ice and cold. I drove home quite gingerly; taking the long way for safety.

The next day my left eye was terribly painful. I flushed it with water and it was turning bright red. Mike took me to Virginia to our ophthalmologist. I had three pieces of black material from the SUV in my eye! The doctor was able to remove them and there was no damage to my eye. Needless to say, we gave tremendous thanks to our faithful Lord.

But there was more glory in this story. While Mike had been shoveling the snow with our neighbor, we had no idea that he had an aortic aneurysm. It was accidentally discovered in a CAT scan several weeks later. Mike had the surgery, and while the doctor was getting ready to remove the aneurysm, which was six times the size of the artery, it was ready to burst. The doctor had to also remove the spleen, but Mike recovered.

Not knowing what any day may bring, I am sure of who is in charge of every day and guards us both personally and with his angels.

❧ JOURNALING ❧

1. *Read Psalm 91.*

2. *Does this Psalm bring you the comfort and assurance you desire in life?*

PEACE, BE STILL

A ugust of 2005 brought incredible angst to my heart, my soul, my body and my spirit. Matt was leaving for Liberty University. After waiting seventeen years to conceive him and then seventeen more years of parenting and enjoying him, we were facing a new, unwelcomed chapter in our lives.

I had just experienced a very serious neck surgery which replaced three discs with cadaver discs. I had a neck fusion and a rod and eight screws placed in C-4, C-5 and C-6. I had to wear a hard neck collar for six weeks. I was not supposed to ride in a car at this time. As a result, I was not able to go with Mike and Matt as they left to get him settled in his new life.

One of my dearest friends came to stay with me. I needed someone who understood and would be able to make me laugh. I was afraid to cry intensely because it could precipitate an asthma attack, and the incision in the front of my throat was quite sensitive, making even the act of swallowing difficult. The thought of sobbing frightened me. I had visions of my having to go to the hospital, so I was determined to control my emotions.

We all prayed together in a circle, and hugged, and said our good-byes. As I watched Matt and Mike leave, I felt such an enormous sword through my heart. As they pulled away, I totally lost it. I collapsed into my friend's arms and sobbed uncontrollably. I had only remembered crying this intensely when my mother died. My friend said later that she had never witnessed anyone cry like this. After what seemed like an eternity, I began to gain control. Then she said, "Not again." Mike and Matt pulled up in front of the house. Mike came back in to get a phone charger for Matt. I waved good bye again and we both melted into big lounge chairs, and spent the weekend watching movies. Comedic relief broke the tension for all of us when I had to call Matt as he was settling in his new dorm to find out how to eject the movie and get the television back to normal. The other new parents in the dorm were also hysterically laughing with my ineptness. My son had to keep repeating which button on which remote to press, and when to press it. Of course with my emotional state, I was not a quick study. It was the first of multiple calls I would make over the years for help with technology.

The weekend passed and Mike came home. We both cried many tears together in the ensuing days. The following week Mike needed to leave for work and asked if I would be alright. I assured him that I was fine. As I began my morning devotions, my eyes naturally looked across the patio to the carport. All at once, I gasped, seeing Mike's car parked there. Matt had been driving Mike's car most of the summer. I jumped off the stool and screamed my son's name. I momentarily thought he was home. Then reality set in. Mike was driving my SUV so that I could drive the car if I had an emergency.

Again I began to sob uncontrollably and realized that I was in trouble. I was alone and having an asthma attack. My throat tightened along with my lungs and the incision in my neck hurt horribly. I cried out to the Lord and said, "Please help me. I am a mother whose heart is broken and I am in big trouble with this asthma attack. Please touch me, for I am all alone and desperate."

What happened next is a cherished memory. All at once, there was warmth that began at that top of my head and slowly descended through my body to my toes. As it enveloped me, the asthma attack ceased and I was conscious of being held and upheld by the Lord in the same spot where Matt had saved my life two years earlier. It was one of those mega-framed moments, where just as the Lord healed so many desperate people in the gospels, he reached out to me and caressed body, soul and spirit. I remain amazed that the Lord God Almighty cares so much for me.

"My soul glorifies the Lord and my spirit rejoices in God my Savior, for he has been mindful of the humble state of his servant."

(Lk. 1:46-48)

❧ JOURNALING ❧

1. Ps. 56:8 tells us that the Lord cherishes our tears, collecting each one in his bottle and recording them in his book. Meditate on this scripture and record your thoughts and impressions.

2. Are you able to cry your heart out to the Lord?

3. Are you willing to let your tears go? You will not drown.

THE BLESSINGS OF A HARD HEAD

T he May of 2012, Matt graduated from Liberty Law School, Magna Cum Laude, much to our delight. He was hired as a staff attorney for Chief Justice Roy Moore. The night before Matt left for Alabama we all decided to retire early. Matt and Mike had already gone to bed and were asleep. Being a woman, it seems to take longer with makeup removal, much to my husband's dismay.

The last thing I remember was washing my hands. I woke up in the shower with my head against the ceramic tile. My body was on the elevated border to the shower. I remember saying, "Margo, what are you doing in the shower?" The next sentence I spoke was, "Oh, my head really hurts."

I got up and walked to the kitchen, got several ice packs, crawled into bed, and fell asleep. This was a terrible decision since I actually had sustained a concussion. Mike didn't hear me fall because he was already deep in sleep. I was unconscious for about fifteen minutes.

The next morning, I got up and covered my forehead with my bangs. I wanted to make Matt's leaving as painless as possible. Mike and I always struggle with sad emotions after Matt leaves. Mike and I worked for the next two hours taking down all of the Christmas decorations. We played all of the wonderfully cheerful Christmas music that we own to help us with our sadness. We took a break and I began to fix lunch. Mike looked at me rather strangely, and asked me if I was feeling alright. That's when I remembered the previous evening's fall. So I pulled back my bangs and Mike's expression let me know that the lump on my head was getting bad. We waited until Monday to see our doctor. My blood pressure which is normally low was sky-high. The doctor said that he believed that my heart had stopped and that I was just lucky that it had started again. I knew it wasn't luck, but that the Lord had his hand on my life for his purposes. My eyes started turning black and the veins in my forehead also turned black. I had sustained a frontal lobe concussion, which can be quite serious.

The week following this episode, Mike and I were watching television and Mike told me, "Margo, I know you know what you are saying, but your sentences are not making any sense." That really frightened me and I prayed silently for full restoration of my frontal lobe.

Five weeks later, at 5:30 a.m., I was again washing my hands and the next thing I knew Mike was standing over me shouting my name. My first thought was, "Why are you yelling at me?" Then I looked around and realized I was flat on the floor. I had passed out again, only this time Mike heard me hit the floor, since he was getting ready for work. He gave me his hand and immediately upon sitting up, I vomited. So we called the ambulance and I was taken to the hospital. I had sustained another concussion. My head had put a hole in the bathroom wall and my coccyx had snapped off. The hospital performed four CAT scans to ascertain the amount of damage. My recuperation took about seven months of horrible pain and limited movement. By the end of July I was able to drive short distances and resume most normal tasks. I needed special pillows in every seat because of the broken coccyx.

One beautiful August afternoon, I drove to the local grocery store and shopped, making sure the bags were not heavily stacked by the cashier. I got home and brought in the first bags of groceries. Upon returning to the car, I was met by an alpha wasp who had decided that the car and contents belonged to his domain. Not to be deterred, I quickly grabbed a can of wasp spray with a twenty-five foot spray. I came back out to the car and confidently took aim. The wasp zigzagged several times. So did my spray. Then all at once, the wasp stopped right in front of me and took aim. In my terror, I thought he looked like Batman. As he flew straight for me, I hurriedly backed up, continuing to spray.

Then it happened! The back of my sandal hit the wall of the carport and my feet flew out from under me. I came crashing down and my heels smacked the concrete. My head bounced twice on the wall of the carport and I know that if my coccyx had not already been broken, I would have broken it with how hard I hit the concrete. I landed in a sitting position. The can of wasp spray was half way across the front lawn.

I sat there wondering if I was alive. I prayed, "Lord, am I broken"? My next thought was, "Can I get up?" I rolled to my side and used a brick column of the carport to pull myself up. I again became well acquainted with ice packs.

I never did see the wasp, but I picture him on the top of the carport laughing hilariously at my predicament that day.

I walked away from this one, as the others, with my brain unscathed, although there are those who might argue with this statement!

The fact that I walked away and can still function fills me with awe at the Lord's protection of his handiwork. I also have acquired a deep appreciation for ice and heat packs.

I had previously gone for EEG treatment in an effort to cure migraines. The doctor who did my brain scan showed me the image. It showed TBI (traumatic brain injury) from two frontal lobe concussions from previous injuries when I was three and five years old in addition to the damage sustained in all of the accidents. The doctor was amazed that I was functioning at such a high level, and that I was able to teach myself piano with all of the complexities involved in reading both staffs of the piano. She told me that I had quite a few 'dings' and that I had really been working my brain very hard to have achieved so much.

All I know for sure is that I have a faithful God who perhaps designed me with an extra thick skull and who has guarded me with unfailing love and faithfulness. I marvel that he has protected my brain throughout all of the physical abuse sustained.

"I will make your forehead like the hardest stone, harder than flint."

(Ez. 3: 9)

❧ JOURNALING ❧

1. *Read Psalm 139. Do you think this Psalm applies to you?*

2. *Explain?*

EZEKIEL'S WHEEL

I had spent most of the summer studying the Minor Prophets. I found myself intrigued by the splendor of Ezekiel's visions and wondered why I had never seen an artistic portrayal of the visions. I had also searched many hours in Christian bookstores that contained art, yet to no avail.

During this time I brought many women with a history of physical, emotional, spiritual, and sexual abuse to a wonderful, Spirit filled pastor. Much ministry was accomplished through this wonderful man who was keenly attuned to the voice of the Holy Spirit.

During one of these sessions, this pastor asked me what I was thinking. I told him that as the other woman was sharing, I was remembering my difficult relationship with my father. He looked deeply into my eyes and told me that I was full of hatred for my father. That revelation stunned me, since I had confronted and made peace with my father while he was still alive. After he prayed, I was told to go to my father's grave and write his name and birthdate on a piece of paper and burn it. I was told to say while it was burning, "It's over, the Lord purges everything through fire," and lastly while leaving the cemetery to quote *Ps. 27:10*, *"Though my father and mother forsake me, yet the Lord will take me up."*

Mike and I went to the cemetery. We took a pot and a book of matches. I took a picture of my father when he was intoxicated and inscribed the back of it. The day was cool and clear and calm. There was no breeze, yet each time that my husband and I attempted to light the picture, covering both the picture and pan with our hands, the flame was extinguished by an inexplicable force. It took us about seven attempts to accomplish the task.

That evening was quiet and restful. I finished getting ready for bed and walked a distance of about seven steps to the bed. Lying down, I placed my head on the pillow, expecting the relief of deep sleep. Immediately upon closing my eyes, I was terrified by a horrible vision. I saw a huge gear, similar in size, to the paddle wheel on a Mississippi steamboat. It was gray and black. I was being uncontrollably pulled toward the crushing gears. I opened my eyes and it was gone. I felt both the pillow and my face, patting both with both hands confirming that I was still awake. I gently closed my eyes and I was again being pulled toward this ominously crushing presence. I opened my eyes and it was gone. I remember getting out of the bed and sitting at the adjacent desk, feeling the desk and my arms and face. Yes, I was entirely awake and not hallucinating. This was not a dream. My husband had fallen asleep and I was wide awake, not dreaming.

Again I lay back down and while closing my eyes, I prayed asking the Lord the meaning of this. Immediately the horrifying wheel was transformed and I was being lifted up within a gloriously sparkling cylinder consisting of thousands of large elongated crystals, the colors of fire. Each was turning independently of the other and somehow they were all being held together by something unseen. Their brilliance was beyond anything on this earth. I remember the terror of being lifted up at a rapid speed and feeling as though I would fall through them and down to my death. I could neither see my body, nor the Lord, yet his presence was there, calming my fears. There was a rushing, roaring, windblown sound present, unlike anything I had ever heard before. This sound is recorded twice by Ezekiel in Chapter 1 as are the mysterious wheels. As the wheel rose higher, I looked down and observed a lush green field partially surrounded by trees. I recognized this as the field behind my childhood home where I believe early abuse occurred. As I looked left, at eight o'clock, I saw a young girl about five years old happily running in place. She had long brown hair and was dressed in a fluffy white dress. I thought it strange that she would be at eight o'clock, since with every migraine I experienced an aura that looked like a sugar-coated doughnut which would evolve into a neon like orb. This aura would become quite vivid and would blind me for about forty seconds. Its intensity would begin at eight o'clock on the circular orb.

This vision of the little girl later reminded me that in the book of Revelation, the overcomers are given white robes. In the vision I kept looking for other children and there were none, only this innocent child lost in the abandon of delightful play.

I drifted off to sleep. When I awoke, I hurriedly recorded the vision. It took me several days to understand that the Lord had shown me his great love. He heard my prayer regarding the illustration of Ezekiel's wheel, but he showed me so much more. He showed me a little girl who had been restored and healed. For years I had led study groups for women who had been physically, emotionally, and sexually abused. He showed me his tender care, his healing, and gave me a glimpse into glory. In Ezekiel's vision, the wheel had many eyes. I often think of the eyes on a peacock's fanned out tail. Since eyes are for the purpose of seeing, I believe that within the glorious wheel I had been allowed to see what the Lord had graciously and lovingly done for me and so many other women who courageously sought their healing.

I believe that the initial crushing wheel was a vision of the destruction of sin and spiritual warfare and the desire of those fallen angels to destroy me. *"The thief comes only to steal and kill and destroy; I have come that they may have life, and have it to the full."* (Jn. 10:10)

"I know a man in Christ who fourteen years ago was caught up to the third heaven. Whether it was in the body or out of the body I do not know—God knows. And I know that this man—whether in the body or apart from the body I do not know, but God knows—was caught up to paradise. He heard inexpressible things, things that man is not permitted to tell."

(II Cor. 12:2-4)

I remain uplifted and filled with praise for this awesome God who went to such an extreme to prove his love for us, dying on a cross to pay for our sins. I also am amazed at how he teaches us through his word and then shows us unimaginable delights. The father heart of God embraces us in our deepest needs and restores the years the locusts have eaten.

"I will repay you for the years the locusts have eaten—the great locust and the young locust, the other locusts and the locust swarm."

(Joel 2:25)

My prayer is that my life will be an ode of praise to this Jesus whom I love.

"I will pour out my Spirit on all people. Your sons and daughters will prophesy, your old men will dream dreams, your young men will see visions. Even on my servants, both men and women, I will pour out my Spirit in those days."

(Joel 2:28-29)

❧ JOURNALING ❧

1. *Do you know the Lord as your personal, good shepherd?*

2. *Do you recognize the movements of the thief (Satan) in your life?*

3. *Has he attempted to destroy you?*

4. *How has Jesus rescued you?*

5. *Read Philip Keller's,* A Shepherd Looks at the 23rd Psalm.

UNEXPECTED ANGEL

I began my morning devotions asking the Lord to give my angels a break, a change of guard around my SUV. I had been through multiple car accidents already and as I prayed that morning, observing my vehicle, I wondered if my protectors were becoming weary.

I drove our son Matt to school that day where I also taught piano and guitar lessons. It was an uneventful day, yet I was weary from keeping up with many little bundles of energy. I was eager to get home and melt into my favorite chair.

The ride home took us along a dangerous, single lane, meanderingly picturesque road. It eventually led to a congested and heavily traveled highway where we waited patiently while facing an unwelcomed and lengthy red light. Our car was first in line at the red light. Every muscle in my body longed for a green light. My every thought echoed 'home.' As that beautiful shade of green beckoned, I deliberately looked to my left for assurance of safety. It was not unusual to see various vehicles barrel through the light, unable to stop. Confident of our safety, I crossed the two southbound lanes, pausing in the median of the highway. I checked again before making my left onto the northbound lanes of the highway. All the traffic had completely stopped for the red light. I confidently proceeded to make the left turn.

Then it happened. As I was in the process of straightening out my vehicle in the right lane of the highway, above my son's head in the adjoining passenger seat, there was a softball sized kaleidoscopic orb. It was iridescent, brilliant and beautiful, consisting of many mesmerizing moving particles. Instinctively, I swerved my vehicle into the left lane. I never looked in my side mirror to see if anyone else was in that lane following me through the light. In the next moment, another SUV ran the red light, traveling well above the local speed limit. We would have been killed. As it sped past us, ever so close, my son saw an angel between our vehicles, protecting us from any impact.

I began to shake uncontrollably and thanked the Lord for our protection. I sped up trying to get the license tag number. My son helped me both to slow down and calm down.

When we pulled into our driveway, we were both praying and thanking the Lord for having been spared. I told Matt what I had prayed in the morning regarding a changing of the guard. I reminded him of *Is. 65:24* where we are told that before we ask, he will answer and while we are still speaking, he would hear. It was a poignant lesson for both of us. Matt had been in the car with me in six of the twelve accidents and he was never harmed. We were spared again. It was a powerful lesson in answered prayer.

❧ JOURNALING ❧

1. *Meditate on Is. 65:24. "Before they call I will answer; while they are still speaking I will hear."*

2. *Does this Scripture encourage your heart? Inspire your prayer life?*

3. *Ask the Lord to grow your awareness of his faithful presence and of his protection.*

THE GOD OF THE FULL CIRCLE

I remain overwhelmingly amazed when I reflect on the loving kindness of the Lord. He graciously breaks through the intensity of our human limitations and gives us breath-taking glimpses of his presence, power and glory.

The last year of her life, my mother was experiencing excruciating pain. I had taken her to my osteopath in Virginia. I feared for her, as her heart was bad and the pain in her back was causing her to grimace, consequently contracting the muscles in her entire body. As we drove, I tried to explain deep breathing, to no avail. Upon arrival, my osteopath also was concerned with how pale her countenance had become. He managed to do some adjustments and the relief was immediate and miraculous. Mom told me that after such intense agony, she couldn't believe that she had total relief. I drove her back home to Maryland and Dad was thrilled. Unfortunately, her relief only lasted for about three hours and then the crushing pain returned. My brother and his wife took her to a local hospital where they admitted her, placing her in traction.

The next day the January weather was unleashing its fury on the metropolitan area in the form of a crippling snowstorm. The government closed early. My brother called me and asked if I wanted to go with him and Dad to the hospital to see Mom. Since I didn't have to drive, I eagerly accepted his invitation.

My mother was resting comfortably in her bed since the medication was controlling the pain. Dad sat to her right, I sat to her left and my brother stood at the end of the bed. All at once, my mother assumed the countenance of a classroom teacher and uncharacteristically yelled at my brother telling him to "get out of the way." She again repeated the order with all of the intensity of a drill sergeant. The three of us looked strangely at each other and my mother. Then she told my brother to "get out of the way, there's a door opening and a hand is reaching out." My brother turned around and patted the wall and told Mom that it was just a wall all the while assuring her that there was no door there. The scenario repeated itself several more times. She insisted there definitely were a door and a hand.

So I quickly exited the room and walked straight to the nursing station. I asked the nurses if she could possibly be hallucinating from medication. I was told that was a possibility. Relaxing, I returned to the room and continued to visit with my mom, dad and brother. By now she had stopped speaking of a door and a hand. After a short visit, we needed to leave the hospital due to the threatening weather. We said our good byes and left Mom who was resting comfortably.

After midnight, we received a phone call from my brother informing us that my mother had just died. We left for the hospital. The nurses were going to leave her in the room until we got to see her again. My mother's body was still warm over her heart. I had to check for myself to be sure that she was really gone. The shock of her unexpected death hit us like a seismic wave. The entire family grieved beyond imagination. Mom had been the heartbeat of our family and her unexpected death caught us all by surprise. The previous June, we had brought my dad home from the hospital in kidney failure. We were all preparing to see Dad die. However, by God's grace, he recovered and lived for another five years.

I was quite angry with myself that I missed Mom's premonition in the hospital, believing it was a drug reaction. The Lord had shown Mom that it was time to come home. Weeks later, Dad told me that he knew he shouldn't have left her that night. My mother had always prayed to die in her sleep. Her mother had prayed the same prayer and my grandmother also died in her sleep.

We all had the same lingering fear—that Mom was not able to reach her nitro inhaler that was on her night stand, because it was placed on the right side and that was the side of her crippled arm. However, reflecting on her vision of the door and the hand, I believe my mother was ready to go home and closing her eyes, woke up face to face with Jesus. The Lord had brought her full circle. In life, she was not able to reach out her arm and hand due to atrophied muscles. In death, the hand of an angel reached out to take her by the hand and lead her home. The Lord had brought her full circle, from infirmity to wholeness.

Several months after Mom's funeral, I went over to visit my dad. As I entered his house, I was immediately struck by the peace and joy that was covering his countenance. I asked him what was going on. He hesitated, speechless. Then he said, "You'll understand because you know the Bible."

He shared with me that he had been in church before Mass and while he was kneeling, he was tapped on the shoulder. He turned to see who was touching him and then he said to me, "She must have been a teenager because she just had short, little wings." She directed my Dad's attention to the altar and what my dad saw next was extraordinary. He saw the altar, filled with glorious angels and in the middle of them all was my mother, floating in a beautiful blue gown. She was smiling and as she floated toward dad, she kept turning both arms palms up and palms down, showing Dad that her right arm was no longer crippled. Then the angel pointed toward the floor near his feet. Dad sat back and lifted up the kneeler. As he related this event, momentarily he was speechless, and his eyes filled with a soft wonder that I had never before seen on his face. He looked me in the eyes and said, "Margo, I saw Heaven!" Excitedly, I asked him to describe what he saw: sights, sounds, colors. Hesitating, he looked at me with full wonder and said, "There are no words." When he looked back toward the altar, the vision was gone.

Dad asked me if I believed him. I told him I did. I told him that in the Bible, angels are sent to minister to us. He responded, "Well she sure did minister to me." Dad asked me if I would tell my brothers and my sister. I shared the testimony and my siblings were filled with awe.

Again, the Lord of the full circle had shown us his sensitivity to decades of our prayers through a vision, involving an arm. This time, my mother was whole and healed. This time, it was her arm that was being seen. This time, my dad was shown that the Lord tenderly cares and hears prayers.

My dad comprehended like never before, the fact that he was forgiven, loved and of great importance to the Lord. My faith, along with my family's, was bolstered. The joy I experience to this day as I recall my father's face, my father's soul caressed by the Good Shepherd, is a treasure more precious than diamonds.

I have been exceedingly blessed by the fact that my father told me to speak and help other women who had been abused. He was able, late in life, to extend blessings to many others, to extend blessings, full circle.

❧ JOURNALING ❧

1. *Have you ever experienced an answer to prayer that took years?*

2. *How did you feel when the answer came?*

3. *Was your faith increased?*

4. *Are you still in the situation where your prayer has not been answered?*

5. *Do you believe that the Lord has your best interest at heart?*

6. *Are you able to trust the Lord even if you never see an answer to your prayer?*

7. *Read Job.*

MORE THAN I COULD IMAGINE

During the summer of 1989, five couples from our former church made the difficult decision to leave and start a church with an emphasis on outreach to the local area. We wanted desperately to spread the good news of the gospel of Jesus Christ, using more contemporary methods of worship and outreach.

The former leadership was locked into traditions and opposed to any suggestions of change. We spoke with them, seeking a resolution to our dilemma. Unfortunately, there was no middle ground. We were told to leave. We held the first meeting of all those interested in the work in our rec room. Sadly, many walked away. They thought our views and ambitions too radical.

We found ourselves abruptly homeless as far as a church body. We were our own little church. We visited about five churches in the region whose worship was patterned after the Willow Creek mega church near Chicago. We had lunch with the pastors, who graciously granted us long and intense afternoons of questions and answers. After the five weeks, we prayed together and believed that the Lord was telling us to move forward. We had found a small room to use for worship in the lower level of the American Legion building.

Eventually, one of our members found a local school that would rent the auditorium to our fledgling group at a reasonable price. We had no air-conditioning and in the winter had to turn off the noisy blowers of the heating system in order to hear the sermons. We slowly grew to 200 people in that school. Everyone gave 150% of time, talents and treasure. We packed up our belongings weekly and stored everything in our trailer locally.

After two years, a new school had been built south of our location and the principal wanted us to rent the auditorium on Sundays. There were several other groups wanting to rent there, but we were granted the lease. In this new location, we grew to 600 over the next six years. Then one of our members, who happened to be a young realtor, made us aware of property that might be available. It was a farm owned by an elderly Jewish man. His singular criterion for selling the property was that the new owners must be people who would give back to the community. Our pastor and elders spent an afternoon with this wonderfully inquisitive man. At the end of the meeting he stated that, "I like you people and I will sell to you."

We worked very hard to raise the money for the deposit on the land. We sacrificed deeply. Even meals at McDonald's were a luxury that needed to be denied. There were no movies, no extras, just prayer and fasting. By God's grace, we raised the money for the down payment. Our anticipation grew as we held picnics and prayer walks on the fifty acres of land. The entire place was bathed in prayer.

Before the building was erected, I remembered a specific prayer that I had dared to pray when we began this venture. *Ephesians 3:20-21* states, *"Now to him who is able to do immeasurably more than all we ask or imagine, according to his power that is at work within us, to him be glory in the church and in Christ Jesus throughout all generations, forever and ever! Amen."* As I meditated on this verse, praying for our new church, I wanted to be specific with the Lord. I remembered that the Scriptures stated, *"You do not have because you do not ask God." (Jas. 4:2b)* So I decided to be bold. Our previous church's greatest growth was 135 people. So I corralled all of my courage and dared to pray for 150 people. That was an enormous church to my numerically-challenged mind.

I had not seen the building during its construction due to medical limitations. The morning of the first service I toured the building in astonishment. As I concluded the tour I entered the sanctuary. The praise team was singing a powerful rendition of "Amazing Grace." I dissolved in tears, collapsing on the shoulders of a precious friend. My eyes were overwhelmed with what I was seeing. That Sunday as the church opened its doors, we had 1,200 people come through the front doors. We were astonished, bewildered, excited, intimidated and delighted all at the same time. Our worship team led us in awesome praise and our senior pastor preached a wonderful sermon. The church continued to grow over the next two years.

Twenty five years later, we have continued in our dream and the Lord had been dramatically faithful to the prayers of our hearts. Needless to say, I learned not to limit the Lord and to pray 'big prayers' to our God who *owns the cattle on 1,000 hills.' (Ps. 50:10)*

❧ JOURNALING ❧

1. *Meditate on Eph.3:20.*

2. *What is your biggest dream?*

3. *Do you believe that God has a bigger dream for you?*

4. *Is he able to enable you to achieve the dream?*

5. *Are you limiting God?*

CONCLUSION

A s I write this book, I am overwhelmed with gratitude and joy for the Lord's plan for my life. I have graphically learned that nothing will interfere with God's plan. There have been many times when I tried to change it, prayed to change it, begged God to change it, but I am so glad that as a loving Father, he did not listen to the rants of a frustrated daughter.

In my life, I have learned that trust is something that is developed and strengthened in the trenches. *"Consider it pure joy, my brothers, whenever you face trials of many kinds, because you know that the testing of your faith develops perseverance. Perseverance must finish its work so that you may be mature and complete, not lacking anything."* (Jas. 1:2-4) I see my life as one that has been, and is still being lived out, in such a sacred romance.

That the Lord of all creation would care so intensely about my life that he would die on a cross for me is totally beyond my comprehension. That he would send his Spirit to live in me as my Counselor, Comforter, and Friend is a concrete reality that fills me with awe and the peace of his abiding, cherishing, and persevering presence.

I look forward to the days that I have remaining on this planet as ones that are opportunities to share his love and glory. My prayer is that everyone on planet earth will come to know him as Lord and Savior.

"For God so loved the world that he gave his one and only Son, that whoever believes in him shall not perish, but have eternal life."

(Jn. 3:16)

❧ Journaling ❧

1. *Read the verse above. (Jn. 3:16)*

2. *Have you ever taken the time to pray, confessing your sins before a holy God and accept his free gift of salvation?*

3. *If not, pray this prayer:*

4. *Lord I confess that I am a sinner and am not worthy to come into your holy presence. I believe that you paid the price for my sins on the cross and that the gift of salvation is totally a free gift. I receive that gift right now. I ask you to fill me with your Holy Spirit. My life is yours. Thank you for such awesome love and forgiveness. Amen.*

WHEN GOD WANTS A MAN

ANONYMOUS

When God wants to drill a man

And thrill a man

And skill a man...

When God wants to mold a man

To play the noblest part;

When He yearns with all His heart

To create so great and bold a man

That all the world shall be amazed —

Watch His methods — watch His ways!

How He ruthlessly perfects

Whom He royally elects!

How He hammers him and hurts him,

And with mighty blows converts him

Into frail shapes of clay which

Only God understands.

While his tortured heart is crying

And he lifts beseeching hands!

How He bends, but never breaks

When his good He undertakes;

How He uses whom He chooses

And with every purpose fuses him

To try His splendor out —

God knows what He's about.

When God wants to take a man

And shake a man

And wake a man...

When God wants to make a man

To do the future's will;

He tries with all His skill...

When He yearns with all His soul

To create him large and whole!

With what cunning He prepares him!

How He goads and never spares him!

How He whets him

And He frets him

And in poverty begets him...

How often He disappoints

Whom He sacredly anoints!

With what wisdom He will hide him;

Never minding what betide him...

Though his genius sob with slighting

And his pride may not forget;

Bids him struggle harder yet!

Makes him so lonely

That only God's high messages shall reach him...

So that He may surely teach him

What the hierarchy planned;

And though he may not understand...

Gives him passions to command.

How remorselessly He spurs him!

With terrific ardor He spurs him

When He poignantly prefers him!

When God wants to name a man

And frame a man

And tame a man...

When God wants to shame a man

To do His heavenly best;

When He tries the highest test

That His reckoning may bring...

When He wants a [god] or king;

How He reins him

And restrains him

So his body scarce contains him...

While He fires him

And inspires him!

Keeps him yearning,

Ever burning

For that tantalizing goal!

Lures and lacerates his soul...

Sets a challenge for his spirit;

Draws it highest then he's near it!

Makes a jungle that he clear it;

Makes a desert that he fear it...

And subdue it, if he can —

So doth God make a man!

Then

To test his spirit's wrath

Throw a mountain in his path;

Puts a bitter choice before him

And relentlessly stands o'er him…

Climb or perish, so He says…

But, watch His purpose — watch His ways!

God's plan is wondrous kind —

Could we understand His mind?

Fools are they who call His blind!

When his feet are torn and bleeding;

Yet his spirit mounts unheeding…

Blazing newer paths and finds;

When the Force that is Divine

Leaps to challenge every failure,

And His ardor still is sweet —

And love and hope are burning in the presence of defeat!

Lo the crisis,

Lo the shouts

That would call the leader out…

When the people need salvation

Doth he rise to lead the nation;

Then doth God show His plan...

And the world has found a man!

Made in the USA
Charleston, SC
16 May 2015